★ **Smoke It** ★
LIKE A PRO
ON THE BIG GREEN EGG & OTHER CERAMIC COOKERS

AN INDEPENDENT GUIDE WITH MASTER RECIPES
FROM A COMPETITION BARBECUE TEAM

ERIC C. MITCHELL

PITMASTER OF THE COMPETITION BARBECUE TEAM YABBA DABBA QUE!
AND CERTIFIED JUDGE BY THE KANSAS CITY BARBEQUE SOCIETY

PAGE STREET
PUBLISHING CO.

PAGE STREET
PUBLISHING CO.

First published in 2015 by
Page Street Publishing Co.
27 Congress Street, Suite 103
Salem, MA 01970
www.pagestreetpublishing.com

The "Big Green Egg" is a registered trademark of Big Green Egg, Inc.

Distributed by Macmillan; sales in Canada by The Canadian Manda Group.

18   17   16   5   6   7   8

ISBN-13: 978-1-62414-098-3
ISBN-10: 1-62414-098-x

Library of Congress Control Number: 201495523

Cover and book design by Page Street Publishing Co.
Photography by Ken Goodman

Printed and bound in USA

Page Street is proud to be a member of 1% for the Planet. Members donate one percent of their sales to one or more of the over 1,500 environmental and sustainability charities across the globe who participate in this program.

DEDICATION

To my wife Cindi, my children Greg and Rebecca,
my mother and father, Madeline and Warren and to all my family,
whether by blood, marriage or smoke.

INTRODUCTION ★ 6

CHAPTER 1 ★ 8

FIRE IN THE HOLE

LIGHTING THE FIRE, SAFETY, TEMPERATURE CONTROL AND SMOKE

CHAPTER 2 ★ 18

LOW AND SLOW

BARBECUING AND SMOKING ON THE BIG GREEN EGG

CHAPTER 3 ★ 50

ROASTING

FROM ALL THAT WALKS, FLIES, SWIMS AND GROWS ABOVE AND BELOW THE GROUND

CHAPTER 4 ★ 108

THE BIG SEAR

GRILLING ON THE BIG GREEN EGG

CHAPTER 5 ★ 130

ONE IN THE OVEN

USING YOUR BIG GREEN EGG AS AN AMAZING CERAMIC OVEN

CHAPTER 6 ★ 158

WET AND DRY

CURING MEAT AND SMOKING ON THE BIG GREEN EGG

CHAPTER 7 ★ 168

DEEP FRYING, GRIDDLING AND WOK-ING AROUND

OTHER GREAT WAYS TO COOK ON THE BIG GREEN EGG

CHAPTER 8 ★ 204

THE INS AND OUTS

CONSTRUCTION, COMPONENTS, ACCESSORIES: USING RUBS, SAUCES AND OTHER CULINARY DELIGHTS

CHAPTER 9 ★ 210

THE TAIL END

CLEANING, MOVING AND TRANSPORTING: COVERS, CARE OF THE WOK, CAST IRON AND DAISY WHEEL

RESOURCES ★ 214

ABOUT THE AUTHOR ★ 215

ACKNOWLEDGMENTS ★ 216

INDEX ★ 217

INTRODUCTION

The Big Green Egg and I have been keeping each other company since the year 2000. We were first introduced by my brother-in-law, Bill Tombari. Bill and his wife Sandy had a pool and outdoor patio where they liked to entertain. When Bill turned 50, Cindi and I wanted to give him something special. After a lot of research, we decided he needed a Big Green Egg so he could entertain by smoking, grilling and baking to his heart's content. Bill loved his Egg and said I should get one, so I did!

I am not a chef, but rather a "food enthusiast." I grew up with a brother, four sisters and thirty-eight first cousins. All my family members are great cooks. Several were farmers, so I grew up on farm-raised meats, fruits and vegetables. Every gathering still centers on family and food.

After I got my first Egg in 2000, I started learning to barbecue, grill and roast meats that I never had before. I was so obsessed that we traveled all the way to Maryland to cook at three Eggfests in Waldorf. We brought back more Eggs!

In 2006, after seeing barbecue competition shows on TV, I asked Cindi to consider entering competition barbecue contests with me. She said yes, so we became certified Kansas City Barbecue Society (KCBS) judges. After judging a few contests, we decided to compete. We became members of the New England Barbecue Society (NEBS). Our first trophy was plastic and was worth $5, but we were hooked! In 2007, we were awarded the NEBS Rookie Team of the Year. Since then, we have won many awards. We've competed twice at the Jack Daniel's Invitational World Championship of Barbecue in Lynchburg, Tennessee, and once at the American Royal Invitational in Kansas City, Missouri.

KCBS contests have four barbecue meat categories: chicken, ribs, pork shoulder and brisket. In New England, many KCBS contests also include a NEBS grilling contest of four categories, such as beef tri tip, Cornish game hen, pizza, wrapped in bacon or dessert. I had never cooked in some of the categories, but as we competed I began to get more comfortable with the Big Green Egg's versatility. We seared steaks, roasted venison tenderloins and baked pies.

For the last several years, Cindi and I have been performing food demonstrations at Big Green Egg dealerships in New England and New York for Tarantin Industries, the Northeast Big Green Egg distributor. We average twelve demos a year. We demonstrate the versatility of the Egg with all we cook.

I trust that this book will bring out your passion for cooking on the Big Green Egg. I have half a dozen Eggs that we use all the time. In fact, everywhere I have a pillow, I have an Egg!

—Eric C. Mitchell

Eric C. Mitchell

CHAPTER 1

FIRE IN THE HOLE

LIGHTING THE FIRE, SAFETY, TEMPERATURE CONTROL AND SMOKE

LIGHTING THE BIG GREEN EGG

Firstly, never use lighter fluid in the Egg! It can soak into the pores of the ceramic, and the smell and the taste will last. For this reason, beware of buying a used Egg; it may have been ruined by lighter fluid.

Before lighting your Egg, stir around any leftover lump to and through the bottom fire grate in order to let any ash settle. I use an ice fishing ice skimmer; you can use a large, perforated metal spoon or the Egg ash tool. Periodically, clean out the vent holes in the side of the firebox to keep them from clogging. Open the bottom vent all the way and rake out the ash into a metal bucket. Make sure the hole in the bottom of the firebox lines up with the vent opening.

Some people start their Eggs with chimney charcoal starters, then dump in the hot, burning lump. I prefer to light the lump in the firebox because it is less messy. I use a hand-held gas torch using Mapp gas. These are hotter than propane; plumbers use them to solder copper pipes! This kind of torch has a self-lighter and can be set to stay burning without your having to hold down a button.

Dump your lump charcoal into the Egg up to the top of the firebox at the bottom of the fire ring. If you are planning to do an overnight cook, load maybe an inch higher but no more. You need to leave room for air to circulate and draft properly.

Unlit charcoal and smoking wood chunks

Adding a plate setter

Drip pan on the plate setter and grid on top

Make three divots in the charcoal in a triangular pattern, always with one in the rear. The egg is always hotter at the rear. Hold the flame in each divot for a minute or so before going on to the next. If the torch goes out while you are holding it in place, it means the fire is getting hot and consuming oxygen. If a flame remains in the charcoal for a few seconds after you remove the torch, close the lid, keeping the daisy wheel all the way open. The Egg dome temperature should be up to 300°F (149°C) in about 10 to 15 minutes. If you need to, burp the Egg (page 12) and hit each spot with the torch again.

Alternative ways to start the Egg are with food paraffin fire starters or with an electric fire starter. You'll still light in three spots in a triangle as described above. Old-school pit masters sometimes use a charcoal chimney starter. To use one, load the unlit lump in the firebox and fill up the chimney. Place the grid on the Egg. Stuff the bottom of the chimney with newspaper and light it, setting it on the grid when lit. When the charcoal in the chimney is well lit after about 10 minutes, remove the grid and dump it in the firebox.

Make sure the fire is going in your three divots before continuing. The entire lump doesn't need to be lit, just three spots. If the fire hasn't spread out enough, it might die out, especially during a long cook. Close the screen all the way on the bottom vent, leaving the bottom vent door all the way open. When the Egg reaches your desired dome temperature for a long cook, add the wood chunks to the charcoal. Add the plate setter, feet up, with one leg in the rear where it is always hotter. Add the drip pan, then the grid. Close the dome but keep the daisy wheel wide open until the Egg comes back up to your desired cooking temperature, then close and adjust it. Let the smoke settle down to a bluish-gray color, and then add your meat. With a big piece of meat, the temperature may drop again. You can open the daisy wheel, then re-set it when the Egg comes back up to the desired temperature, providing the smoke does not get too heavy.

If the weather isn't very warm—say, below 75°F (24°C)—and you are not adding wood chunks or chips, you can overshoot the desired cooking temperature by 25°F to 50°F (13°C to 28°C) before adding the plate setter, drip pan and grid. Once the dome is closed, the temperature will drop back near your desired temperature. Adjust the daisy wheel and add your food when the temperature has climbed back up to the desired dome temperature. If it is too hot out (more than 75°F [24°C]), sneak up to your desired temperature and do not overshoot before putting in the plate setter, drip pan and grid. Adjust the vent to the desired temperature, and when it's corrected, add the food.

A NOTE ON INDIRECT VS. DIRECT HEAT

The Egg is set up for indirect roasting, meaning that the heat is not directly below and exposed to the food. Indirect roasting allows for more even cooking than direct grilling, where the underside of your roast is very hot and the top not as hot. You can grill many things directly, but it requires much more time and more attention to flipping and turning, not to mention opening the Egg dome more often. There is a saying in barbecue: If you are lookin', you ain't cookin'. By roasting indirectly, you allow the the heat to stay more consistent, which allows the roast to cook more evenly.

An indirect cook is accomplished by placing a heat shield above the charcoal with a grid above it. The most popular shield is a Big Green Egg plate setter. It is placed on top of the fire ring with the three legs pointing upward. For roasting, you can put a foil-lined drip pan on the plate setter, then place a grid on the plate setter legs. This technique raises the grid so it's about level with the dome gasket. If you don't have a plate setter, use a pizza stone or your drip pan as a shield. For this method, you need one grid on top of the fire ring and another above the drip pan. I have sometimes used bricks to support the second grate.

SAFETY

Cooking on the Big Green Egg requires learning how to keep yourself from getting burned, as well as food safety procedures. The Egg is not dangerous, but when it's open, you're dealing with an open flame. Just like you need to be careful around your fireplace or woodstove, you need to be careful around your Egg.

Always keep gloves readily available. I use leather welder's gloves to open the Egg and to handle all the tools, accessories and components. I buy them at a local discount store, and when they get too stiff to use, I buy another pair.

The number one concern in Egg safety is planning for and avoiding flashback. Flashback happens when the Egg dome is opened: fresh oxygen becomes available to the charcoal, which explodes into a ball of fire. The most common time for flashback is when you close the Egg vents down on a hot fire. Closing the vents helps lower the temperature, but it starves the fire for air. At that point, if you open the dome too soon, flashback can occur. To combat flashback, always "burp" your Egg. Burping allows a smaller amount of air to the charcoal so that it doesn't get too much air all at once. To burp your Egg, slowly lift the dome about 3 inches (7.5cm), wait a couple of seconds then slowly open it all the way. Never let anyone who doesn't know about burping open the Egg. Flashback is less likely to occur when the Egg is below 300°F (149°C), but it can still happen, especially right after the plate setter is added and the fire has not yet settled down. When you're checking the temperature of oil for deep-frying, burp the Egg and leave the dome open. Wearing a heat proof glove, remove the cover from your Dutch oven or frying pan and check the temperature of the oil. If it is less than you need, replace the cover, close the Egg and check again in a few minutes.

Second, be aware that, when you have a hot fire and you add big meats and close down the vents, the draft can immediately reverse, causing flames to shoot out the bottom vent. Flames can cough out even when the screen is closed. Embers can shoot out, too, so always use the bottom vent screen. I open the screen only when starting the Egg, to allow for more air flow; but when the Egg starts heating up on its own, to a dome temperature of about 250°F (121°C), I close the screen.

Third, always use a drip pan when rendering fat, and make sure it's deep enough. If the grease gets too deep in your drip pan while you're cooking, carefully empty it. Do not use a disposable aluminum pan, as it might melt. Flashback can set the drip pan grease on fire. If this happens, close the dome and all of the vents to starve the flames. Then beware of flashback when you re-open the dome.

Fourth, keep a heat-resistant spot in your cooking area to cool down a hot grid or plate setter, or simply to put them down for a minute while rearranging the inside of the Egg.

Now for food safety. Always use a food thermometer to make sure your food is thoroughly cooked before you serve it to family, friends—or judges. I always use an instant-read thermometer, such as Thermapen from ThermoWorks. You can use dial thermometers, but the instant-read keeps my hand from getting too hot, and it makes it necessary to open the dome only briefly. Safe serving temperatures after resting are 165°F (74°C) for ground turkey, chicken and other poultry; 160°F (71°C) for ground beef or pork; 145°F (63°C) for beef steaks, pork chops, fresh pork and ham, and seafood. Check temperature in several areas, especially the thickest part, and especially with poultry. Keep cooked food above 140°F (60°C). It must be cooled to 41°F (5°C) within four hours to be safe. If re-heating, heat to at least 165°F (74°C).

When handling raw meat, wash your hands well and often. I can't always do this, so I use powder-free latex gloves. If you choose to wear gloves, change them often: dirty gloves are as bad as dirty hands.

Also be aware of cross-contamination. Raw chicken should never be stored above other foods, it might drip on them. Do not let raw chicken in your ice cooler sink into the ice water. When cutting chicken, never re-use cutting boards or utensils without washing and sanitizing them. If you wear gloves when handing raw chicken, change them.

Raw meat and fish should smell clean. If they don't, they've gone bad. When in doubt, throw it out! The exception is large cuts like beef brisket, pork butts and especially pork ribs, which can have an "off" smell when removed from the vacuum sealed packaging. This smell can be caused by physical changes that occurred during vacuum sealing, but not necessarily spoilage. Rinse the meat thoroughly under cold water. If the smell goes away, you are all set.

TEMPERATURE CONTROL

Temperature control of the Big Green Egg works like that of a wood stove or a fireplace. Air comes into the fire and is controlled by a damper above the fire. If you open it, the fire gets hotter; if you close it, the fire subsides. Air comes in through the bottom vent, through the burning charcoal, then up into the dome and out the top vent. I prefer to control the temperature by opening and closing the daisy wheel on the top vent. I leave it wide

Daisy wheel wide open

Daisy wheel wide open

Daisy wheel closed with petals open

open until my desired temperature is reached. I leave the bottom vent wide open, too, with the screen closed. I was instructed a long time ago to adjust both the top vent and the bottom vent, keeping them equally open. After many long cooks, during which I went up and down the stairs all night to adjust each vent, I abandoned that method. I now adjust only the daisy wheel, leaving the bottom all the way open with the screen closed. For longer cooks, once the Egg has settled down at my desired temperature—I wait about an hour—I set the daisy wheel one last time and go to bed without the worry that my competition meats may not cook correctly. I wouldn't do it this way if it weren't reliable.

Eggs of every size function the same. The time they take to heat up, however, varies with the size. For example, the medium Egg comes up to temperature faster than the large, and the large faster than the extra large. The more mass to heat up, the longer they take.

ACHIEVING TEMPERATURE

The daisy wheel on top of the Egg slides all the way open for maximum draft and highest temperatures. The top also spins, creating oval-shaped openings which look like daisy petals. When the top is closed, you adjust the amount of air that gets in by changing these petal openings. You can tighten or loosen the nuts on the daisy wheel to make adjustments easier or more difficult. The following adjustments work for lower temperatures:

Petals wide open	300°F (149°C)
Petals ½ open	250°F to 275°F (121°C to 135°C)
Petals ¼ open	225°F (107°C)
Petals slightly open	190°F to 200°F (88°C to 93°C)

To cook at higher temperatures, slide the daisy wheel top open to permit more airflow. When the top is all the way open, the petal openings don't matter. The following adjustments work for higher temperatures:

Slide ¼ open	325°F to 400°F (163°C to 204°C)
Slide ½ open	425°F to 550°F (218°C to 289°C)
Slide ¾ open	575°F to 700°F (302°C to 371°C)
Slide all the way open	725°F and above (385°C and above)

It is easier to hold temperatures below 375°F (191°C) than to hold higher temperatures. When you slide the top open, the temperature rises quickly because the charcoal is getting more oxygen. Higher temperature settings should be monitored more closely than when the daisy wheel slide is closed and the petals are open. Do note that petal holes may not be perfectly shaped, or they may not line up perfectly, so just average the amount that they're open.

Increasing the temperature in the Egg is easier than lowering it. Because the ceramic is a great insulator, it cools very slowly. You can reduce the fire by closing down the vents, but the dome temperature might stay hot for a long time. When you are planning to cook multiple foods, try to do your high temperature cooks last, or spread out the cooks of individual foods so the Egg has time to cool down. You can reasonably get the Egg down from 700°F (371°C) to 400°F (204°C) by closing the top and the bottom vents, and maybe putting the rain cap on, until the temperature drops near your desired setting. If the outside temperature is 70°F (21°C) or below, this could take between 20 and 30 minutes. If the temperature is above 80°F (27°C), it will take much longer. Be extremely cautious of flashback when you are reducing the temperature. The dome temperature may be coming down, but if you open the Egg, the fire, which is still very hot and starved for oxygen, can easily erupt. Wear heat-resistant gloves and burp the Egg slowly. Cooling the Egg down is discussed at the beginning of Chapter 4 (page 108).

My recipes always refer to dome temperature because it is what I use and it's where the thermometer is located. For indirect cooking, grid-level temperature will usually be less than dome temperature. I take this differential into account when I am cooking a multilevel cook. Food at the grid level will cook more slowly than food up in the dome. I move food around as necessary.

The dome temperature may drop when you add the plate setter and large meats, especially in a low-and-slow cook. The temperature will come back up in a few minutes. If it doesn't, open the top vent to provide more airflow and draft until you get back to your cooking temperature, then reset the daisy wheel.

Calibrate your dome thermometer regularly. To do this, take the thermometer out of the dome and put a pair of pliers on the nut under the dial. Place at least 1 inch (1.3 cm) of the thermometer tip into boiling water and see whether it reads 212°F (100°C). If it doesn't, hold the dial with a cloth and rotate it until it is at 212°F (100°C). It may take a couple of tries before you get it calibrated.

Many people use other temperature probes, electronic thermometers and fan temperature controls. I don't anymore. If you want to have more evidence on how your cook is going, or if you want to sit inside and monitor the cook on your laptop, go ahead! But just setting the daisy wheel works well for me. It's up to you. Heck, there are some out there who say that, if you aren't cooking on a stick burner, then you can't cook barbecue!

Some environmental factors can affect temperature control on the Egg. On a very hot day, the Egg will cool down more slowly. If it is windy, with 20mph (32kph) gusts, the draft can be interrupted or reversed. A wind gust may suck air out of the bottom vent or top vent. In these conditions, I keep the bottom vent opened the same amount as the daisy wheel.

If your charcoal is wet or has picked up moisture, it will not get as hot as you need it to, regardless of how much the vents are open. Either discard it or dry it in the sun.

Two environmental factors that do not affect the Egg temperature are rain and cold. If your Egg is up to temperature, its superior insulation qualities will allow your cook to continue unhampered. However, during cold weather, always place a stick the size of a pencil between the dome and the bottom before you cover your Egg after your cook because the gasket can freeze shut. I know this from experience. However, a frozen Egg has never kept me from cooking ribs on Super Bowl Sunday, especially when the Patriots were playing!

I like my food cooked on the Egg to be smoked but not smoky. The right amount of smoke adds a subtle flavor, but too much smoke or bad smoke will ruin a good cut of meat or fish. Have you ever prepared to put a bite of barbecued food in your mouth, and just before it hits your lips your nose twitches, your tongue runs backwards, you get ready to cough and a slight tear comes to your eye? This is an encounter with too much smoke! If you take a bite anyway and the back of your throat cracks and dries out, you've had some bad smoke. These problems stem from using smoke that's too strong, along with smoking too long and not letting the billowing smoke settle down to a bluish-gray wisp.

All-natural hardwood lump charcoal is made from hardwood, but not always the same hardwood. The denser the lump, the less smoke it gives off, and the longer it lasts with less ash. Softer lump, which is usually less expensive, gives off more smoke, burns faster and leaves more ash. The brand of lump charcoal you use makes a difference. I prefer Wicked Good Charcoal. It takes more effort to light than other charcoals, but it is worth it. If I must use another charcoal, I will monitor the fire more closely. The Naked Whiz has a charcoal database with ratings and reviews (page 214, Resources).

When I use hard lump, I can decide which wood chunks or chips to add to it to create the smoke. I do not soak chunks, and I don't add too many. For a long cook, I usually use three, and I add them when the Egg comes up to my target temperature. I let them smolder until the smoke dies down to a bluish-gray color, 10 to 15 minutes. I don't use chunks for short cooks, nor do I use chips. I let the minimal smoke from the lump do the smoke flavoring. You may decide to use chips. If you do, soak them first for at least an hour and let the smoke settle down the same as if you were using chunks, before adding your meat.

The type of wood chunks or chips you use makes a difference in the smoke you get. Hickory and mesquite can be very strong. Personally, I think mesquite is too strong. I prefer hickory for use with big cuts of beef and pork. I find pecan a bit less smoky and good for all big meats. Fruitwoods like apple and peach go well with pork and poultry and are a little sweeter. Cherry and maple are similar, and can also be used with beef. Cherry will even add a little red color.

How much smoke you like and what kind of charcoal, chunks or chips are matters of personal preference. Just don't start out too strong, or you might have regrets. Anything cooked on the Egg with a little smoke comes out much better than in the oven!

CHAPTER 2

LOW AND SLOW

BARBECUING AND SMOKING ON THE BIG GREEN EGG

Barbecue is often called "low and slow": low temperatures over a long period of cook time. Temperatures usually range between 200°F and 275°F (93°C and 135°C). Grilling, by comparison, is hot and fast: higher temperatures for a shorter period of time. Barbecue is not only about the low and slow cooking method, but also about the social gathering that surrounds cooking outdoors and feeding many hungry and chatty people! Often, barbecues involve grilling meat hot and fast, not low and slow. It doesn't matter the method; it is still a barbecue. You wouldn't call it a "grilling," would you? Grillings only happen when you stay out way too late or you've been invited "down to the station." Grillings aren't pleasant.

Most barbecue meats are cheap because they are tough. They are the opposite of tenderloin. The best way to get barbecue meats tender is to cook them at a low temperature for a long time, so the outside doesn't burn before the center is tender. Big meats, like beef brisket, beef or pork ribs and pork shoulder must cook for a long time before the collagen and connective tissues dissolve and the meat becomes incredibly tender. The flavor is always there, but if the meat isn't tender, your teeth, jaw bone and tongue get worn out from chewing before you can taste anything. Barbecue, however, changes everything.

The process is simple. Build a fire; add wood chunks for smoke flavor; rub the meat with a flavorful dry rub; cook indirectly at a low temperature and wait! The wait is the only hard part. Before I started competition barbecue, I cooked my pork butts for 20 to 22 hours at about 200°F (93°C) on one load of lump. The irresistible smell of the meat cooking would penetrate the neighborhood. Walk around a barbecue competition at five in the morning, and the aromas are heavenly! At the Greenfield, Massachusetts competition, I met a police officer from the South who had just gone off duty at 7 a.m. When he opened the station door a half mile away from the competition site, he smelled the barbecue and followed his nose right to the competition!

Barbecue is cooked over indirect heat with a drip pan in the Egg. The setup is the same as for roasting, except the dome temperature is in the range of 225°F to 275°F (107°C to 135°C), depending on the meat, and the cook is longer. Pork butt and beef brisket can cook at a dome temperature of 250°F (121°C) for about 10 hours, depending on their size and whether you foil the meat, which I will discuss next. Ribs can cook at a dome temperature of 250°F (121°C) for 4 to 5 hours, depending also on the size of the racks and whether you foil.

I mentioned earlier that I used to cook pork butts for over 20 hours. They came out great! In competition, however, I don't have the luxury of time. I will therefore cook at a higher temperature and will use foil to speed up the cook time. Some purists refer to wrapping in foil as "the Texas crutch." Crutch or not, I find that foiling will yield outstanding results; most competition cooks use it. The meat will be cooked at 160°F (71°C), but won't be tender until it reaches 190°F to 200°F (88°C to 93°C). After the meat reaches about 160°F (71°C), its internal temperature will plateau for hours until all the collagen and connective tissue have dissolved. The internal temperature rises ever so slowly, but the meat is still cooking and going through a physical change, which takes time. Foiling will speed up the process; and I believe—as do the judges—that it can give perfect results. When I foil, I double wrap the meat and add a little liquid before sealing up the foil and returning the meat to the Egg. I use a beef-flavored juice for beef, and fruit juice for pork.

After about an hour, brisket, pork and ribs should reach about 190°F to 200°F (88°C to 93°C) and pass the plateau. At this point, I wrap foiled pork or brisket in a towel and place it in an empty cooler to rest for several hours, or at least one hour. Ribs don't need to rest and can be unwrapped and placed back on the Egg at a dome temperature of 300°F to 350°F (149°C to 177°C) for about half an hour. Sauce, if desired, can be added in the last 10 to 15 minutes to glaze the ribs. The same applies for the brisket flat, but make sure to reserve the broth from the foil for dipping. When adding sauce, keep the dome temperature below 350°F (177°C) to prevent the sugar in the sauce from burning.

Pork shoulder can be taken out of the foil and pulled, chopped or sliced, with some of the broth from the foil added, as well as a little sauce. The recipes that follow give more specific directions for barbecuing different cuts of meat.

By the way, for all indirect cooks, I use the dome temperature. The dome temperature in the Egg for indirect heat can be 15°F to 30°F (8°C to 16°C) more than the grid temperature because of the way the heat convects around the plate setter and up past the grid into the dome. The longer the cook, the less the differential. A low and slow cook will be at a lower temperature for a longer time, allowing the grid temperature to rise nearly to the dome temperature. I use the dome temperature because that is where the thermometer is, so I don't need to open the Egg. This is analogous to controlling the Egg temperature only with the daisy wheel top vent, leaving the bottom vent open and screened. Checking the grid temperature is one extra step I personally do not use. The dome temperature reference works well. Why keep track of two temperatures when one will do?

COMPETITION BOSTON PORK BUTT

I love pig butts and I cannot lie! The butt end of a full shoulder is commonly called "Boston Butt." It isn't from the butt of the pig, but from the top part of the front shoulder. The lower part is the "picnic." The two sections have different muscle structures. When both sections are attached, they're called a full pork shoulder. For the Kansas City Barbecue Society (KCBS) pork shoulder category, most pit bosses choose the Boston Butt. Other sanctioning organizations, such as the Memphis Barbecue Network (MBN), require the whole shoulder to be cooked.

I love the butt because of its versatility. For competition barbecuing, I choose an 8- to 10-pound (3640 to 4500g) bone-in butt. You can use de-boned butt, but I find that the meat near the bone has the best texture and flavor, and it cooks evenly, bone in. When the butt is deboned, some of the good meat is scrapped with the bone and it is harder to barbecue evenly with so many muscle parts disconnected. However, boneless pork butt is great for other types of cooking recipes, such as Buckboard Bacon (page 165) and Garlic Sausage Fatties (page 74).

MAKES 20 TO 24 SERVINGS

1 (8- to 10-pound [3640 to 4500g]) bone-in pork butt

¼ cup (60ml) yellow mustard

1 cup (120g) Pork Rub (page 208)

½ cup (120ml) apple juice or apple cider

¼ cup (60ml) pork marinade (such as Stubb's Pork Marinade®), strained

¼ cup (60ml) maple syrup

½ cup (120ml) barbecue sauce

When choosing a competition pork butt, find one that is relatively square with a consistent thickness. Opposite the bone end is the "money muscle." It is called the money muscle because, when cooked correctly and sliced separately to put in the "turn-in" box at competitions, it has a great pork flavor and a soft but not mushy texture that will melt in your mouth. For competition, it's money!

The money muscle is a separate, tube-shaped muscle about 1½ to 2 inches (4 to 5cm) in diameter. The part you can see is more pink than deep red and has very narrow bands of fat along the tube, about 1 inch (2.5cm) apart.

The butt will have a fat cap on the top and no fat on the bottom. Trim down the fat cap to about ¼ inch (6mm). Feel the underside of the entire butt with the tips of your fingers to check for bone shards that may have been left during butchering. Remove any bone pieces and sinew.

For competition, I partially separate the muscle pieces around the bone end, starting from the bottom, using my fingers to break the connective tissue, going side to side to push apart the muscle. Next, using a boning knife, I remove the membrane that once connected all the the muscles. Cleaning out the membrane gives more surface to add rub and eliminates the need to peel off the cooked membrane prior to turn-in. When you do this, be careful not to completely separate the muscles! In competition cooking, pork butt must be cooked whole, not separated. On the opposite end of the butt, partially separate the muscle the same way. There is usually some very hard fat at one end of the muscle, which should also be removed.

(continued)

COMPETITION BOSTON PORK BUTT (CONTINUED)

Add a slather of prepared yellow mustard to all exposed meat, including the crevices. The mustard will hold the rub and will not leave any flavor once the pork is cooked. Generously rub the butt, including crevices, with pork rub. Now it can be wrapped and refrigerated for several hours until ready to barbecue.

Set the Egg for 275°F (135°C) indirect with a drip pan, filling with charcoal to the top of the firebox. With the top and bottom vents wide open, light the fire and close the Egg. When the dome temperature gets up to about 250°F (121°C), about 10 minutes, close the bottom screen. When the dome temperature approaches 275°F (135°C), about 5 minutes, slide the top of the daisy wheel closed, leaving the petals halfway open.

Prior to adding the meat, put in three chunks of hickory and two chunks of pecan. Initially, there will be very white, billowing smoke. This is bad, bitter smoke! Wait until the smoke has settled down to a softer, bluish-gray color, then add the butts to the grate, fat-side up. Close the dome and cook at 275°F (135°C) until the internal temperature reaches 160°F (71°C), about 8 to 10 hours for an 8-to 10-pound (3640 to 4500g) butt. Smaller butts will take less time. Remove from the Egg and place fat-side up on a double layer of aluminum foil. Wrap foil tightly and add ½ cup (120ml) apple cider before closing the wrap. Replace the foiled butt back on the Egg and continue to cook at 275° (135°C) indirect for 1½ to 2 hours, until the internal temperature reaches 195°F (91°C). You can probe through the foil to check the temperature. At 195°F (91°C) internal, remove from the Egg, open the foil and add ¼ cup (60 ml) pork marinade, strained and mixed with ¼ cup (60ml) maple syrup. Re-foil, wrap the butts in a couple of towels and place in an empty cooler to rest and keep warm. The meat will stay above 140°F (60°C) for a couple of hours if wrapped.

When ready to turn in, unwrap and slice off the money muscle. Remove the bone and then pick out the muscles. Place the chunks, with bark, in barbecue sauce. Slice the money muscle into ¾-inch (2-cm) slices and pull apart the other muscles. Place the whole, sliced money muscle into the turn-in box and add a pile of pulled and chunked pork.

COMPETITION PORK RIBS

I love pork ribs. I used to eat them wherever I could: at buffets, at chain restaurants, at Mom-and-Pop restaurants and even in the Caribbean at roadside *lolos*. Most ribs served at chains and buffets are steamed or boiled for tenderness, then grilled for crispness. I never knew how much flavor I was missing until I cooked them on the Egg. I have become a rib snob. I no longer eat ribs that haven't come off a Big Green Egg! I prefer to eat pork ribs "dry"—with no sauce in the cooking process—as opposed to "wet," in which the ribs are basted in sauce. You will taste more pork flavor dry. Sauce can always be served on the side.

For Kansas City Barbecue Society (KCBS), the pork rib category can include pork spare ribs, St. Louis cut spare ribs or baby back ribs. I prefer the St. Louis. This cut is spare ribs trimmed so that the rack is rectangular. One end will be as wide as the longest bone, about 6 inches (15 cm), and the other end, where the shorter bones are, will have some of the meat without bones in it. On the bone side of the slab, the thin meat flap that is near the knuckle of the shorter bones will be removed. Baby back ribs are cut up higher, nearer the back bone, and have good meat, but less of it. St. Louis have much more meat and great flavor.

MAKES ABOUT 9 SERVINGS

3 racks St. Louis-cut spare ribs

½ cup (120ml) prepared mustard

1 cup (100g) Pork Rub (page 208)

3 sticks unsalted butter, sliced

½ cup (120ml) honey

¾ cup (177ml) apple cider, divided

Remove the two outer membranes on the bone side of the ribs, but leave the one attached closest to the bone and meat. You can remove the outer, thicker membrane by grasping it with a paper towel and peeling it from the bone tips down to where the flap was. The membrane removal works best if the ribs are very cold. Sometimes the membrane has already been removed during the butchering process, so don't stress out trying to remove it if you can't find it. On the meat side of the ribs, remove any thick fat between the bones. Remove the layer of fat and sinew on the short-bone end of the rack, exposing the rib meat. Trim any meat hanging from the end of the cut bones to give a very even appearance. Remove any sharp bone pieces from the end of the rack. Rub the racks with yellow mustard and then with pork rub on both sides. You can then wrap the ribs and place them in the refrigerator for a few hours until you're ready to cook.

Set the Egg for 250°F (121°C) indirect with a drip pan. The firebox should be almost full with charcoal. With the top and bottom vents wide open, light the fire and close the Egg. When the dome temperature gets up to about 200°F (93°C), about 10 minutes, close the bottom screen. When the dome temperature approaches 250°F (121°C), about 5 minutes, slide the top of the daisy wheel closed, keeping the petals halfway open. Once the fire is lit, add two chunks of maple and one chunk of fruitwood—apple, cherry or peach—and close the lid.

Once the smoke has settled down to a bluish-gray color, add the ribs, either bone-side down on the grate side by side, or on the thin side in a vertical rib rack. Cook for 3 hours, turning and rotating every 45 minutes. (Do not flip the slabs if they are lying flat on the grate; just rotate them).

(continued)

COMPETITION PORK RIBS (CONTINUED)

After 3 hours, place the racks on a double layer of aluminum foil, meat side down. The foil should be coated with a layer of butter, drizzled honey and sprinkles of rub. Wrap each rack tightly in the foil and add ¼ cup (60 ml) of apple cider to each rack prior to wrapping completely. Place foiled ribs back on the 250°F (121°C) Egg, meat-side down, and stacked if necessary, for another hour. Rotate and change the stacking order a couple of times. After an hour, the wrapped ribs should be very limber when held by the ends. Remove from the foil and place on the grate, meat-side down, and sauce the bottom. Flip and sauce the meat side. Leave on the Egg for 15 or 20 minutes for the sauce to set. If you don't have grid space for all of the racks, remove them in pairs from the foil and sauce them two at a time until they are all glazed. Using an extended rack will allow you to glaze four racks at a time in a large Big Green Egg.

Once they're glazed, let the cooked ribs rest, tented in foil, on a drying rack for about 10 minutes. To cut, place them meat side down on a cutting board and slice between the bones. Slicing them bone side up allows you to see the bones better, as they will change direction farther down the slab. Serve meat side up.

If you want to cook many racks of ribs on the Egg at one time, a vertical rib rack from Big Green Egg can hold six full racks on their side on the large Big Green Egg. You can add more ribs by adding a second layer above the first and by cutting the racks in half. A three-tier adjustable rack from the Ceramic Grill Store can hold six racks lying flat. When the Egg is stuffed with ribs, you will need to rotate them and move them around often to help them cook evenly. When you wrap them in foil, they can be stacked on each other and shuffled during the one-hour wrapping period. It is harder to glaze a lot of racks because they glaze best when lying flat. If you take them out of the foil to firm up and then place them on the Egg the same way you started your cook, you can heat the sauce and serve on the side, or brushed on and not glazed. These are going to be the best ribs your guests ever ate, however you serve them. If you want to cook even more racks, buy another Egg. Don't laugh; many Eggheads do!

COMPETITION BEEF BRISKET

Brisket is the toughest part of the cow. Some refer to it as "chunk-o'-chest." Every time the animal moves, walks, runs, sits, lies down or rolls over, the brisket muscles are being used. It's a tough cut, but when barbecued correctly, it is one of the most tender and flavorful pieces of beef. The cut has two parts, the flat and the point. The grains run differently in each and there is more fat and connective tissue in the point. Together, they make up a "full packer" brisket. You can barbecue either cut separately, for shorter cooking times, but I prefer to cook the full packer brisket whole, and then separate it before serving.

MAKES 20 TO 24 SERVINGS

1 (14-pound [6.35kg]) full packer beef brisket

2 cups (475ml) injection, optional (I mix ½ cup [60 g] of Butcher BBQ Original Injection with 2 cups [475 ml] water)

¼ cup (60ml) yellow mustard (if not using injection)

1 cup (120g) Beef Rub (page 208)

2 cups (475ml) Rick's Sinful Marinade (page 30)

The top of the brisket has a thick fat cap. The underside, showing mostly the flat, has little fat showing. There is a thick layer of fat between the point and the flat. To prepare, trim any visible fat off of the flat bottom and slice any sinew off the bottom, slicing along the surface with the grain. On the top fat cap, cut most of the fat away except for a quarter of an inch (6 mm) on the flat portion. On the point, all of the fat on the top can be removed.

Once the meat is trimmed, you can opt to inject it. Inject the flat with the grain; the point can be injected at any angle. Be careful, as injecting brisket can be very messy. You can never predict where or when the injection will make a break for it! When you're finished injecting, rub any injection on the surface evenly onto the brisket, then coat with beef rub. If you're not injecting, then coat with mustard and then the beef rub. The brisket can be wrapped and refrigerated for a few hours until you are ready to barbecue.

Set the Egg for 250°F (121°C) indirect with a drip pan. Fill the charcoal to the top of the firebox. With the top and bottom vents wide open, light the fire and close the Egg. When the dome temperature gets up to about 200°F (93°C), about 10 minutes, close the bottom screen. When the dome temperature approaches 250°F (121°C), about 5 minutes, slide the top of the daisy wheel closed, keeping the petals halfway open. When the Egg is up to temperature, add two chunks of hickory and one of pecan.

When the smoke has settled down and is bluish gray, about 10 minutes, add the brisket, fat side up, with the point to the rear, near the hinge. Close the dome and smoke for 8 to 9 hours, until the internal temperature is above 160°F (71°C). Set the brisket on top of a double layer of aluminum foil, fat side down, and wrap tightly. Before closing one end, add a couple of cups (475 ml) of Rick's Sinful Marinade. Place back on the Egg at 250°F to 300°F (121°C to 149°C) until the internal temperature reaches 190°F to 200°F (88°C to 93°C) and the thermometer slides in and out with a little resistance, about 30 minutes to an hour. Remove from the Egg and open the top of the foil at the point end. Wearing heat-resistant gloves, carefully

(continued)

COMPETITION BEEF BRISKET (CONTINUED)

slice through the fat layer between the point and the flat, separating them. Set the point in a half pan and save it for burnt ends (page 32). Close the foil around the flat, wrap in a towel and place in an empty cooler to rest for a couple of hours.

As I stated earlier, brisket is a very tough cut of meat. For competitions, I cook two whole packers, each the same way, and one is always better than the other. Both are good, but one is maybe a bit more tender or juicy. The brisket is done when it reaches 190°F to 200°F (88°C to 93°C) internal, but I also probe the meat with my thermometer to see how easily it goes in. You can probe right through the foil. If the temperature is 190°F (88°C) and the probe slides easily, the brisket is done. If the probe slides with difficulty, let the meat cook towards 200°F (93°C) internal. You should try to get it to 160°F (71°C) internal before you wrap. If you are short on time, you can speed up the cook by increasing the Egg dome temperature to 350°F (171°C) after wrapping. On the other hand, if your brisket is done early, it will last for a few hours foiled, wrapped in a towel and placed in a dry cooler. Just make sure the internal temperature stays above 140°F (60°C). If necessary, place it back on the cooker, still in the foil. I believe the brisket will still turn out the best following the times and temperatures in the recipe, but the above corrections will still yield very good results.

When you're ready to serve, trim away remaining fat from the flat, and place it back on the Egg at 250°F (121°C) direct or indirect, saucing each side. After about 10 minutes total, remove from the Egg and slice the flat across the grain into ¼-inch (6mm) thick slices. Drizzle some of the liquid from the foil over the slices.

RICK'S SINFUL MARINADE

This isn't a true marinade, but a liquid to use when you wrap your brisket in foil. It is from Rick Salmon, a well-known barbecue aficionado on all of the online forums. Double this recipe to make the correct amount for two briskets.

YIELD: 4 CUPS (945 ML), ENOUGH FOR 2 (14 POUND [6.4 KG]) BRISKETS

1 (12-ounce [355ml]) can of beer

½ cup (120ml) apple cider vinegar

½ cup (120ml) water

½ cup (120ml) Worcestershire sauce

¼ cup (60ml) olive oil

1 tablespoon (18g) beef base

2 tablespoons (30ml) barbecue sauce

1 tablespoon (7g) seasoned salt or rub

1 tablespoon (7g) celery seed

1 teaspoon (2g) cayenne pepper

1 teaspoon (3g) MSG (optional)

Heat all ingredients before using, to help them dissolve. Then simply combine them in a small bowl.

COMPETITION SMOKED CHICKEN

Competition chicken is smoked over a lower heat for a longer time than grilled chicken. The perfect result for smoked chicken is a tender and juicy bite with a light flavor of smoke, rub and sauce. You should be able to bite through the skin. While whole chicken, or any part of the chicken, can be turned in with or without bones, bone-in smoked thighs are the most popular chicken among competition pit masters. In my opinion, they are juicier than breast meat and have more flavor. At the Jack Daniel's World Championships in Lynchburg, Tennessee, teams are required to turn in both white and dark meat. Many teams choose to turn in smoked wings and thighs.

MAKES ABOUT 6 SERVINGS

9 chicken thighs, bone in, skin on

12 ounces (355ml) unsalted chicken broth

½ cup (60g) Chicken Rub (page 209)

2 sticks unsalted butter, cut into 9 pieces each

Barbecue sauce (optional)

Select large thighs that are the same size so they will be finished at the same time. Carefully remove the skin and cut away any fat or silver skin. With a knife or kitchen shears, cut all pieces into the same shape, keeping as much meat as possible. Lay the skin on a cutting board, inside up, and carefully scrape as much fat off of the skin as possible, using a boning or a chef's knife. Be careful not to cut through or rip the skin. After scraping, place the skin back on the trimmed thighs, tucking the skin under. Trim away any excess. The key is to have enough skin tucked under the thighs that it will stay put when placed on the grid. The tedious skin scraping is what you hope will lead to bite-through skin, which is what the judges are looking for. Inject about 1 ounce (30ml) of salt-free chicken broth on each side of the thighbone. After injecting, lift the skin and add rub to the meat. Replace the skin and add rub to the outside of the skin. The prepared chicken can now be refrigerated for a few hours until you are ready to barbecue.

Set the Egg for 250°F (121°C) indirect with a drip pan. With the top and bottom vents wide open, light the fire and close the Egg. When the dome temperature gets up to about 200°F (93°C), about 10 minutes, close the bottom screen. When the dome temperature approaches 250°F (121°C), about 5 minutes, slide the top of the daisy wheel closed, keeping the petals halfway open.

In an aluminum half pan, spread 9 pats of unsalted butter. Place your chicken thighs on the pats of butter, skin side up. Add an additional pat of butter on the top of each thigh. When the fire is going, add a couple of chunks of pecanwood and a chunk of applewood. When the smoke has settled down to a bluish-gray color, about 10 minutes, add the pan of chicken, close the dome and cook until the internal temperature reaches 140°F (60°C), about 1 hour. Flip the thighs in the pan, skin side down, in the butter bath and continue cooking until the internal temperature reaches 160°F (71°C), about 15 minutes more. Remove the thighs from the pan and place them skin side up on an indirect grid. Add rub to the skin and cook for an additional 10 to 15 minutes, or until the rub caramelizes on the skin and the internal temperature of each thigh reaches at least 165°F (74°C). Remove from the Egg and tent with foil on a drying rack; let rest for 10 minutes before serving.

BEEF BRISKET BURNT ENDS

While pork butt is my favorite cut to cook, properly barbecued brisket burnt ends are the best thing I have ever tasted coming off of the Egg. They melt in your mouth, with a crunchy bark on the outside and a juicy inside.

MAKES ABOUT 8 SERVINGS

3 pounds (1360g) cooked brisket point

½ cup (120ml) reserved brisket juice (page 27)

⅛ cup (15g) Beef Rub (page 208)

¼ cup (60ml) barbecue sauce

Take a cooked brisket point and trim away any remaining fat. Cut into 1-inch (2.5-cm) cubes and season with beef rub. Place the cubes in a 9 by 12-inch (23 by 31-cm) baking pan, or an aluminum half pan, with reserved liquid from the brisket flat.

Set up the Egg at 250°F (121°C) indirect. With the top and bottom vents wide open, light the fire and close the Egg. When the dome temperature gets up to about 200°F (93°C), about 10 minutes, close the bottom screen. When the dome temperature approaches 250°F (121°C), about 5 minutes, slide the top of the daisy wheel closed, keeping the petals halfway open.

Place the half pan with the brisket on the grid, lid closed, for about 1 hour. Coat each cube with your favorite barbecue sauce and cook for another 20 to 30 minutes, until they are well glazed. Remove from the Egg, keep your own stash and then serve to others (if there's any left).

Note: If the fat and connective tissue in the cooked point are still a little bit chewy, cook longer before adding the barbecue sauce.

BABY BACK RIBS

Baby back ribs are cut from the high part above the pig's rib cage, below the spine and loin muscle. They are also called "loin back" or "back ribs." The bones are more consistent in size than spare ribs, which are lower in the rib cage. There is more meat within the back rib bones than in the spares. The meat is leaner, having less fat than other cuts of the pig. Baby back ribs are the rave at restaurants and on T.V. They cost more than spare ribs, but are still good eats. For an alternative, try with a peach preserve glaze instead of barbecue sauce.

MAKES ABOUT 12 SERVINGS

4 racks baby back ribs

¼ cup (60ml) prepared yellow mustard

½ cup (50g) Pork Rub (page 208)

Butter, honey and additional rub for the foil

¼ cup (60ml) apple juice

½ cup (120ml) barbecue sauce (Dare you go dry?)

Remove the membrane from the bone side of the rack, just like with spare ribs (page 24). Trim any meat hanging from the end of the cut bones to give a very even appearance. Rub the racks with yellow mustard, then rub with pork rub on both sides. These can be wrapped and placed in the refrigerator for a few hours until you're ready to cook.

Set the Egg for 250°F (121°C) indirect with a drip pan. The firebox should be almost full with charcoal. With the top and bottom vents wide open, light the fire and close the Egg. When the dome temperature gets up to about 200°F (93°C), about 10 minutes, close the bottom screen. When the dome temperature approaches 250°F (121°C), about 5 minutes, slide the top of the daisy wheel closed, keeping the petals halfway open. Once the fire is lit, add two chunks of maple and one chunk of fruitwood: apple, cherry or peach.

Once the smoke has settled down to a bluish-gray color, add the ribs either bone side down on the grate side by side, or on their thin side in a vertical rib rack. Cook for 2½ hours, turning and rotating every 45 minutes. Do not flip the slabs if they are lying flat on the grate; just rotate them. After 2½ hours, place the racks on a double layer of aluminum foil, meat side down. The foil should have a layer of butter, drizzled honey and sprinkles of rub. Wrap each rack tightly in the foil and add ¼ cup (60ml) of apple juice prior to wrapping completely. Place foiled ribs back on the 250°F (121°C) Egg, meat side down and stacked, if necessary, for another hour. Rotate and change the stacking order a couple of times. After an hour, the wrapped ribs should be very limber when held by the ends. Remove from the foil and place on the grate, meat side down, and sauce the bottom. Flip when sauced and sauce the meat side. Leave on the Egg for 15 or 20 minutes for the sauce to set. If you don't have grid space for all the racks, remove them in pairs from the foil and sauce them two at a time until they are all glazed. Using an extended rack will allow you to glaze four racks at a time in a large Big Green Egg.

After glazing, let the ribs rest, tented in foil, on a drying rack for about 10 minutes. To cut, place them meat side down on a cutting board and slice between the bones. Slicing them bone side up allows you to see the bones better, as they will change direction farther down the slab. Serve meat side up.

LO'-N-SLO' BBQ ROASTED TURKEY

This recipe was contributed by the Lo'-N-Slo' Barbecue Team of Tom and Michele Perelka, and their German Shepherd Sky, from New Providence, Pennsylvania. They earned a fourth-place rib call at their first official contest in 2006 and have been hooked ever since. They have earned 15 Grand Championships, 14 Reserve Grand Championships, 2 grilling and more than 275 top-ten category calls. Earning an invitation to the Jack Daniel's World Invitational, they finished second place in the Cook's Choice category. They returned to Lynchburg in 2010 and earned a first place Cook's Choice with a perfect 180 score. At the Jack in 2014, they won first place chicken! Their team has been named the Pennsylvania State BBQ Champions in 2011, 2012, 2013 and 2014, as well as the Mid-Atlantic BBQ Association's Pennsylvania State Cup Champions in 2011. Cindi and I have competed against them at many contests, and they are a big part of our barbecue family.

MAKES ABOUT 12 SERVINGS, PLUS LEFTOVERS

1 (12- to 14-pound [5.4-kg to 6.3-kg]) turkey

FOR THE BRINE

½ gallon (2L) apple cider

1½ cups (432g) kosher salt (they like Morton's Coarse®)

1½ cups (330g) dark brown sugar

1½ cups (355ml) agave

1 cup (237ml) apple cider vinegar

½ cup (120ml) orange juice

¼ cup (60ml) lemon juice

¼ teaspoon ground cloves

¼ teaspoon poultry seasoning

1 tablespoon (8g) whole black peppercorns

6 bay leaves

FOR THE HERB BUTTER

1 stick (113g) unsalted butter, softened

3 cloves garlic, minced

1 tablespoon (3g) minced fresh rosemary

1 tablespoon (3g) minced fresh thyme

1 tablespoon (3g) minced fresh oregano

1 tablespoon (3g) minced fresh parsley

1 tablespoon (3g) minced fresh sage

FOR THE STUFFING

1 orange, cut into 8 wedges

1 lemon, cut into 8 wedges

1 lime, cut into 8 wedges

1 apple, cut into 8 wedges

1 medium onion, cut into 8 wedges, skin on

4 cloves of garlic, slightly crushed, skin on

4 sprigs fresh rosemary

Small bunches of parsley, oregano and thyme

4 sage leaves

(continued)

Make the brine 4 or 5 hours before you plan to brine the turkey: combine all ingredients in an 8-quart (8L) pot; bring to a boil over high heat, stirring occasionally. Remove from the heat and add 8 cups (2L) of cold water, stirring well. Cool to room temperature and refrigerate until cold.

Once the brine is cold, place turkey, breast side down, in a tub or pot large enough to hold it and the brine. Add the brine and refrigerate 8 to 12 hours. Remove the turkey from the brine; rinse and dry; discard brine. Place turkey on a tray and refrigerate, uncovered, for 3 hours, to help dry the skin so it gets crispier when cooked.

Make the herb butter by placing the softened butter in a bowl and mixing together all ingredients.

Remove the turkey from the refrigerator. Carefully slide your hands under the skin to loosen it from the breast meat. Spread the herbed butter directly on the breast meat with your fingers, being careful not to tear the skin. Stuff the body and neck cavities with wedges of orange, lemon, lime, apple, onion, garlic and herbs.

Place the turkey in a roasting pan. Fill a resealable bag with ice and place it on the breast meat. Allow the turkey to rest on the counter for 1 hour. This process chills the white meat to help it cook as slowly as the dark meat.

Preheat the Egg to a dome temperature of 350°F (177°C), with plate setter legs up. With the top and bottom vents wide open, light the fire and close the Egg. When the dome temperature gets up to about 250°F (121°C), about 10 minutes, close the bottom screen. When the dome temperature approaches 350°F (177°C), about 5–10 minutes, slide the top of the daisy wheel partially closed, keeping it ¼ open.

Place a 9-inch (22-cm) round cooling rack directly on the bottom of the plate setter to elevate the roasting pan. Place lidded roasting pan, containing turkey, on top of the 9-inch (22-cm) cooling rack. Close the dome and cook at a dome temperature of 350°F (177°C). After 1½ hours, remove lid. If there is not a lot of liquid in the bottom of the roasting pan, add some liquid—water, turkey broth, white wine, etc. Continue cooking until the instant-read thermometer registers 165°F (74°C) in the breast. This will take 1¼ to 1½ hours depending on the size of the turkey. Remove the roasting pan from the Egg and let rest 15 to 20 minutes. Remove stuffing, carve and serve.

MARYLAND-STYLE PIT BEEF

Maryland pit beef sandwiches are great! Roasting your own pit beef on the Egg makes them even better because it will be smokier and juicier than any you can buy. You can cook several smoked roasts at once and refrigerate for later.

MAKES 10 SANDWICHES

1 (4-pound [1814g]) boneless top sirloin roast
2 tablespoons (30ml) olive oil
¼ cup (30g) Beef Rub (page 208)
1 recipe Tiger Sauce (page 39)
10 Kaiser rolls
1 onion, thinly sliced

Trim any fat from the roast and rub with olive oil, then with the beef rub.

Set the Egg for 300°F (149°C) direct. With the top and bottom vents wide open, light the fire and close the Egg. When the dome temperature gets up to about 250°F (121°C), about 10 minutes, close the bottom screen. When the dome temperature approaches 300°F (149°C), about 5 minutes, slide the top of the daisy wheel closed, keeping the petals open all the way. When the Egg is up to temperature, add a chunk of hickory.

Once the smoke has quieted down to a bluish-gray color, place the roast directly on the grate and sear on all sides for about 2 minutes per side. Once it's seared, remove the roast from the Egg and prepare the Egg for 300°F (149°C) indirect with a drip pan. Place the roast back on the Egg, close the dome and cook until the internal temperature of the roast reaches 120°F (49°C). Remove from the Egg, tent with aluminum foil and let rest for 15 minutes.

While the roast is resting, mix the Tiger Sauce ingredients together. Slice the rolls in half, then slice the meat very thinly and across the grain. A meat slicer or an electric knife works well for this. Spread Tiger Sauce on both the top and the bottom of the sliced roll. Fold a few slices of beef onto the bottom of the roll, add 2 slices of onion, and add the top of the roll to serve.

(continued)

TIGER SAUCE

YIELD: 1 CUP (240 ML)

½ cup (120ml) mayonnaise
½ cup (120g) prepared horseradish
1 tablespoon (9g) minced garlic
1 teaspoon (5ml) lemon juice
½ teaspoon salt
½ teaspoon black pepper

In a small bowl, combine all ingredients.

BARBECUED JERK CHICKEN

Cindi and I have been to the Caribbean several times. Every time we go, I have to taste a bite of jerk chicken. When I'm not there and I taste good jerk chicken, I can close my eyes and be teleported there, with the sunshine, warm breezes and friendly people. Jerk chicken originated in Jamaica, where jerk seasoning was originally used for pork. With all of the aromatic spices and seasonings, the chicken picks up some of the apple smoke flavor as well. If you weren't content enough, the habañero will add an additional "Oh yeah!"

MAKES ABOUT 6 SERVINGS

6 chicken pieces, bone in

1 habañero pepper, seeds and ribs removed, diced

½ cup (76g) chopped green onion

1 tablespoon (9g) minced garlic

1 tablespoon (9g) minced ginger

2 teaspoons (4g) nutmeg

1 teaspoon (5g) allspice

1 teaspoon (2g) cloves

1 teaspoon (2g) dried thyme

1 teaspoon (2g) black pepper

1 teaspoon (2g) cinnamon

½ teaspoon salt

Juice from one lime

Juice from one orange

2 tablespoons (30ml) white vinegar

1 tablespoon (15ml) vegetable oil

Jicama Salad (page 106)

Wash the chicken pieces and pat dry. Mix all of the dry ingredients together in a large bowl (down through the salt). Add the liquid ingredients and mix until well blended. Rub each piece of chicken with this marinade paste, both on and under the skin. Refrigerate the coated chicken and any remaining paste for 4 hours or overnight.

Set the Egg for 250°F (121°C) indirect with a drip pan. With the top and bottom vents wide open, light the fire and close the Egg. When the dome temperature gets up to about 200°F (93°C), about 10 minutes, close the bottom screen. When the dome temperature approaches 250°F (121°C), about 5 minutes, slide the top of the daisy wheel closed, keeping the petals halfway open. Add two chunks of applewood.

When smoke is diffused and bluish gray, about 10 minutes, add the chicken parts, skin side up, to a well-oiled grate above a drip pan. Close the dome and cook for about 45 minutes, until each piece reaches at least 165°F (74°C) internal temperature, flipping and rotating a few times. When finished, remove from the Egg and let rest for 10 minutes under tented aluminum foil over a drip pan. Serve with jicama salad.

SMOKED HAM

Although ham is already fully cooked, and sometimes smoked, the second smoking with the liquid rub adds several layers of flavor. Because the ham is fully cooked, you do not have to cook it long to get a high temperature. Your guests don't need to know you didn't cook it from scratch: the flavors from the smoke and the liquid rub will pleasurably fool them all!

MAKES 15 TO 20 SERVINGS

1 (8-pound [3.6kg]) fully cooked, bone-in ham

½ cup (115g) dark brown sugar

½ cup (120ml) maple syrup

2 tablespoons (30ml) dark brown mustard

1 tablespoon (3g) black pepper

Set up the Egg for 250°F (121°C) indirect. With the top and bottom vents wide open, light the fire and close the Egg. When the dome temperature gets up to about 200°F (93°C), about 10 minutes, close the bottom screen. When the dome temperature approaches 250°F (121°C), about 5 minutes, slide the top of the daisy wheel closed, keeping the daisy wheel petals halfway open.

Remove any skin from the ham and trim any fat cap down to about ¼ of an inch (6mm). Score the surface in a diamond pattern, 1 inch (2.5cm) apart and about ½ an inch (1.5cm) deep. In a medium bowl, mix all of the ingredients together, then rub the mixture all over the ham, including into the score marks. When the Egg reaches 250°F (121°C), add one chunk of hickory and one chunk of applewood.

Once the smoke has died down and turned bluish gray, place the ham on the Egg, close the dome and roast to an internal temperature of 120°F (49°C), about 1½ hours, turning every 30 minutes. When cooked, remove from the Egg and tent in aluminum foil on a rack to rest for 10 minutes. Slice and serve.

BARBECUED BEEF BACK RIBS

Beef back ribs are cut from the more expensive cuts of beef, such as prime rib and rib eye. Make sure you buy meaty ribs that have not been overly trimmed. Beef back ribs can be tough, but when slow cooked, the connective tissues and cartilage melt away, leaving juicy, beefy ribs. Just like brisket point, when cooked low and slow they will be crisp on the outside and will melt in your mouth.

MAKES 10 TO 12 SERVINGS

5 pounds (2.2kg) beef back ribs

2 tablespoons (30g) yellow mustard

½ cup (100g) Beef Rub (page 208)

6 ounces (180ml) dark beer

1 tablespoon (15ml) Worcestershire sauce

Remove the membrane from the back of the ribs. Rub both sides of the rack with yellow mustard, then add beef rub to both sides, using more on the meaty side.

Set up the Egg for 250°F (121°C) indirect with a drip pan. With the top and bottom vents wide open, light the fire and close the Egg. When the dome temperature gets up to about 200°F (93°C), about 10 minutes, close the bottom screen. When the dome temperature approaches 250°F (121°C), about 5 minutes, slide the top of the daisy wheel closed, keeping the petals open halfway. When the Egg is up to temperature, add two chunks of wood, one hickory and one cherry.

When the smoke has settled down and is a bluish-gray color, place the racks on the Egg, meat side up. Close the dome and cook for 3 hours, rotating every hour. Remove from the Egg and place meat side down on a double layer of aluminum foil. Wrap tightly and add the dark beer and Worcestershire sauce before closing the last end. Place back on the Egg, meat side down, for one hour or until the meat between the bones reaches an internal temperature of 200°F (93°C). Remove from the foil and place back on the Egg, meat side up. Add a bit more rub and cook for an additional 15 minutes. If you wish to add barbecue sauce, cook an additional 15 minutes to glaze over. When finished, remove from the Egg and let rest under foil tent on a drying rack for 10 minutes. Place on a cutting board, meat side down and cut between the bones. If cooked dry, serve the barbecue sauce on the side.

(continued)

BIG GREEN EGG PASTRAMI

Pastrami is smoked corned beef. Corned beef is brine-cured beef brisket. Making pastrami is one step more than barbecued beef brisket. You know how much I love pork, and pastrami is the beef version of bacon, sort of. It takes time to cure, but it is well worth the wait!

MAKES ABOUT 12 SERVINGS

5 pounds (2.2kg) brisket flat

FOR THE BRINE

8 cups (2L) water

¼ cup (50g) dark brown sugar

4 teaspoons (20g) curing salts (I like Morton's Instant Cure™)

1 tablespoon (9g) ground coriander

1 tablespoon (9g) pickling spice

¼ cup (60ml) minced garlic

2 tablespoons (18g) fresh ground black pepper

FOR THE DRY RUB

4 tablespoons (36g) fresh ground black pepper

2 tablespoons (18g) coriander powder

Add the brine ingredients to the water and bring to a boil, then simmer for one hour. Remove from the heat and let cool to room temperature, then place in the refrigerator to cool to 40°F (5°C) or less.

Trim all but ⅛ inch (3mm) of the fat cap off the brisket. Using a non-reactive covered container, or plastic freezer bags, cover the brisket with the cooled brine. If using plastic bags, it is best to double them up. If the brisket is too large for the container or bag to lie flat, cut the brisket in half and use two bags or containers. Place the brisket with brine in the refrigerator for 5 to 10 days, turning twice a day.

Remove from the brine and rinse off any brine pieces. Pat dry.

Mix the dry rub ingredients together and press them into the brisket to cover. Mix more if necessary.

Set up the Egg for 250°F (121°C) dome indirect with a drip pan. Fill the firebox to the top with charcoal. With the top and bottom vents wide open, light the fire and close the Egg. When the dome temperature gets up to about 200°F (93°C), about 10 minutes, close the bottom screen. When the dome temperature approaches 250°F (121°C), about 5 minutes, slide the top of the daisy wheel closed, keeping the petals halfway open.

When the Egg is up to temperature, add three chunks of wood: one pecan and two apple or cherry. When the smoke has settled down and is a bluish gray, place the brisket on the Egg, close the dome and cook until an internal temperature of 160°F (71°C) is reached, about 5 hours (less for a smaller cut). Remove from the Egg and place on a double layer of aluminum foil. Fold tightly and add ¼ cup (60ml) water before closing. Place the foiled brisket back on the Egg at dome temperature 250°F (121°C) and cook until an internal temperature of 190°F (88°C) is reached, about 1 hour. Wrap in a towel and place in an empty cooler to rest for 1 to 2 hours before slicing across the grain, or refrigerate overnight to aid in slicing.

SLOW ROASTED PORK STEAKS

I've said it before: I think pork butts are the best and most versatile part of the pig, even better than bacon. Pork steaks are sliced, bone-in pork butts. Because of their thinness, they cook up relatively quickly. They are like giant pork chops, but juicier and more tender. Ask your butcher to slice a whole pork butt for you. They are both the tastiest and the cheapest part of the pig—a two-fer!

MAKES ABOUT 4 SERVINGS

4 pork steaks

2 tablespoons (30ml) prepared yellow mustard

¼ cup (30g) Pork Rub (page 208)

1 cup (240ml) apple cider or apple juice

Wipe any bone dust off the steaks and pat dry. Slather with mustard and then add pork rub to each steak.

Set the Egg for 250°F (121°C) indirect with a drip pan. With the top and bottom vents wide open, light the fire and close the Egg. When the dome temperature gets up to about 200°F (93°C), about 10 minutes, close the bottom screen. When the dome temperature approaches 250°F (121°C), about 5 minutes, slide the top of the daisy wheel closed, keeping the petals halfway open.

When the Egg is up to temperature, place the steaks on the grate, close the dome and cook until they reach an internal temperature of 200°F (93°C), about 2 hours. Turn and flip the steaks every half hour and spray them with apple cider to keep them moist. When the steaks are done, remove them from the Egg and let them rest for 10 minutes, tented under aluminum foil. Serve!

CINDI'S SLAW

This is a fast and easy slaw recipe that adds a sweet crunch to pulled pork sandwiches or pork egg rolls and makes a good side dish for a variety of barbecue dishes. It feeds a crowd. It's a great dish for a pot luck or outdoor gathering because it doesn't need to be refrigerated.

MAKES 10 TO 12 SERVINGS

1 (3-pound [1.3kg]) bag of shredded cabbage mix

1 medium onion, diced fine

1 green bell pepper, diced fine

2 cups (400g) granulated sugar

½ cup (120ml) olive oil

¼ cup (60ml) white vinegar

¼ cup (60ml) apple cider vinegar

1 tablespoon (7g) celery seed

1 teaspoon (2g) mustard seed

In a large bowl, combine cabbage mix, diced onion and diced bell pepper and mix well. Sprinkle the sugar over the top.

In a small saucepan, heat the olive oil, vinegars, celery seed and mustard seeds. Simmer for 2 minutes to blend the flavors. Pour over the cabbage mix and stir to partially dissolve the sugar. Cover and refrigerate. Let the slaw marinate for at least 2 hours, stirring occasionally. It can marinate overnight, but make sure you stir the ingredients well the next morning. Strain the slaw to remove the liquid and you are good to go!

CHAPTER 3

ROASTING

FROM ALL THAT WALKS, FLIES, SWIMS AND GROWS ABOVE AND BELOW THE GROUND

When you think about roasting on a Big Green Egg, think of it as a brick oven with a smoke flavor component from the charcoal. You can roast in a conventional oven, but you will not add any subtle smoke flavor, and will be roasting in a much drier environment than in the Egg. The Egg's moisture retention is far superior to that of a conventional oven, without the use of a water pan. I never use water in the Egg. It's not necessary and will discourage the caramelization and crisping of the food you are cooking.

The Egg is set up for indirect roasting, meaning that the heat is not directly below and exposed to the food. Indirect roasting allows for more even cooking than direct grilling, where the underside of your roast is very hot and the top not as hot. You can grill many things directly, but it requires much more time and more attention to flipping and turning, not to mention opening the Egg dome more often. There is a saying in barbecue: If you are lookin', you ain't cookin'. By roasting indirectly, you allow the the heat to stay more consistent, which allows the roast to cook more evenly.

An indirect cook is accomplished by placing a heat shield above the charcoal with a grid above it. The most popular shield is a Big Green Egg plate setter. It is placed on top of the fire ring with the three legs pointing upward. For roasting, you can put a foil-lined drip pan on the plate setter, then place a grid on the plate setter legs. This technique raises the grid so it's about level with the dome gasket. If you don't have a plate setter, use a pizza stone or your drip pan as a shield. For this method, you need one grid on top of the fire ring and another above the drip pan. I have sometimes used bricks to support the second grate.

I mentioned laying your roast on the grid that you've placed on the legs of your plate setter. For best results, add an extended grid on top of this grid to raise the roasting environment so it's centered and higher—we say, "up in the dome." You want to have everything in your Egg centered so that the heat will come up evenly around the shield, then up and around and under the roast. If you roast just on the grid resting on the plate setter legs, there will be less heat on the underside of the roast and more heat on top. With any setup, you need to rotate and flip the roast a few times because there is a natural hot spot in the rear of the Egg. I always put one leg of the plate setter in the rear to mitigate the hotter temperature there. If you are roasting big and small items, the larger items should go to the rear of the Egg. If you are roasting several items at once, go ahead and use all the grid levels.

When I cook indirectly, I always use a drip pan lined with foil on the plate setter to catch drippings and melted fat. Clean up is easy, as you can throw the foil away after cooking. The drip pan will be dirty and will never be used for baking again, but by adding new foil before your next indirect cook, you can make it last forever. If you don't have a drip pan, you can make one by curling up the sides of a piece of aluminum foil. Be careful! If you have a lot of grease and fat, it might leak onto the charcoal and cause a grease fire. If this happens, close the dome and the top and bottom vents and wait a few minutes before burping and opening the Egg. When you are done cooking, you can leave the drip pan and the used foil in the Egg until it has cooled down, avoiding any possibility of spilling grease on the fire.

I generally start the Eggs the same way for all cooks. Chapter 1 (page 11) describes when to add wood chunks or chips and at what temperature to add the plate setter, drip pan, grid and your roast.

The Egg is very easy to use. It only takes a little practice and minimal patience to learn what to do when and how to improvise, if necessary. The biggest factor, which comes naturally, is passion. We wouldn't be Eggheads if we didn't have great passion for cooking on the Egg!

GRILLED ASIAN MARINATED PORK BELLY

This pork belly is very tasty and can be eaten as grilled, or placed in a taco or wrap. The flavor is mildly sweet and spicy and the texture is very soft. Ask your butcher or visit an Asian market for fresh pork belly. If it comes with the skin on, save the skin for Pork Cracklin's (page 192).

MAKES ABOUT 24 SERVINGS

3 pounds (1.3kg) uncured boneless pork belly, skin removed

6 cloves garlic

¾ cup (180ml) soy sauce

9 tablespoons (113g) dark brown sugar

6 tablespoons (90ml) sesame oil

3 tablespoons (45ml) rice wine vinegar

3 teaspoons (15ml) chili oil

1½ teaspoons (2g) hot pepper flakes

5 green onions, sliced

Toasted sesame seeds

Slice the pork belly into strips about ⅛ inch thick (3mm) that are about 3 inches (7.6cm) long. Mix all of the other ingredients together through the hot pepper flakes and place in a nonreactive container or thick resealable plastic bag. Placed sliced pork belly in the marinade and refrigerate for 12 to 24 hours, turning occasionally.

Set up the Egg for 350°F (177°C) indirect with a drip pan. With the top and bottom vents wide open, light the fire and close the Egg. When the dome temperature gets up to about 250°F (121°C), about 10 minutes, close the bottom screen. When the dome temperature approaches 350°F (177°C), about 5-10 minutes, slide the top of the daisy wheel partially closed, keeping it ¼ open.

Add the meat to the grid and close the dome. Grill indirect for 10 minutes, turning once, until meat is cooked through. Serve with sliced green onions and sesame seeds on top.

GRILL-ROASTED PORK BRACIOLE

Pork braciole is an excellent way to cook my favorite meat, pork shoulder. Traditionally, braciole is made with beef, top round or flank steak, seared then braised in a tomato sauce for several hours. This recipe grills the pork and creates a slightly smoky flavor with a well-blended filling that has different textures and flavors. This is a must try!

MAKES 6 TO 8 SERVINGS

2 pounds (900g) pork shoulder or boneless country-style ribs from shoulder

4 ounces (120g) salami, sliced then chopped

¼ cup (40g) pepperoncini, drained and minced

¼ cup (40g) minced garlic

¼ cup (30g) dried, Italian-style bread crumbs

¼ cup (5g) chopped fresh parsley

½ cup (90g) shredded Parmesan cheese

2 tablespoons (30ml) olive oil, divided

1 teaspoon (6g) salt

1 teaspoon (2g) black pepper

In a medium bowl, mix together the chopped salami, minced pepperoncini, minced garlic, bread crumbs, chopped parsley and Parmesan cheese until well combined.

Slice the shoulder into ½-inch (1.5-cm) slices, about 3 to 4 inches (7.5 to 10cm) wide and 6 to 8 inches (15 to 20cm) long, with the grain running the long way as much as possible. If using boneless ribs, butterfly them to a ½-inch (1.5-cm) thickness. Lay the slices between plastic wrap and pound them with a meat mallet to about a ¼-inch (6-mm) thickness, being careful not to tear the meat. Remove the top piece of plastic wrap, salt and pepper the top of the pork and rub in 1 tablespoon (15ml) of olive oil on the slices. Divide the salami and cheese mixture into equal portions and spread on each slice, pressing the mixture into the pork. Starting with the slice nearest you, roll each slice like a jelly roll. Tie the rolls with wet butcher's twine at 1-inch (2.5-cm) intervals. Rub the outside of each roll with the remaining olive oil, and salt and pepper each roll. Refrigerate rolls until ready to cook, up to 24 hours.

Set up the Egg for 350°F (177°C) direct on a raised rack. With the top and bottom vents wide open, light the fire and close the Egg. When the dome temperature gets up to about 250°F (121°C), about 10 minutes, close the bottom screen. When the dome temperature approaches 350°F (177°C), about 5-10 minutes, slide the top of the daisy wheel partially closed, leaving it ¼ of the way open.

Place braciole rolls on an oiled grid, close the dome and cook, turning often, until the internal temperature reaches 180°F (82°C), about 30 minutes. If the outsides of the rolls begin to char too much, switch to an indirect cook. When done, remove from the Egg and let rest for 5 to 10 minutes under a tent of aluminum foil on a rack. Once they have rested, snip off the butcher's twine and serve, cutting into medallions.

CHEESY STUFFED CHICKEN BREAST

Chicken breasts are universal favorites because they are very lean, but they often become dry or tough. This recipe helps solve the problem two ways. First, a marinade is made not only to add flavor, but to help the meat retain a little moisture while cooking. Second, and most importantly, if you follow this recipe, you will not overcook the meat. Chicken must be cooked all the way through, especially when rolled, but not beyond 165°F (74°C) internal. By being cooked indirectly, the stuffed breast cooks more evenly and stays moist. Slightly smoky chicken, cheese and vegetables, plus spices, create a moist, flavorful bite with different textures and flavors.

MAKES ABOUT 4 SERVINGS

4 boneless, skinless chicken breasts
2 tablespoons (30ml) olive oil, divided
Salt
Pepper

MARINADE
¼ cup (60ml) lemon juice
½ cup (120ml) orange juice
2 tablespoons (30ml) olive oil
2 tablespoons (19g) chopped garlic
¼ cup (60ml) soy sauce
1 teaspoon (3g) onion powder
1 teaspoon (2g) black pepper
1 tablespoon (5g) dried thyme

STUFFING
½ cup (50g) chopped mushrooms
2 tablespoons (20g) chopped shallots
1 tablespoon (9g) minced garlic
½ cup (121g) cream cheese, softened
¼ cup (45g) grated Parmesan cheese
¼ cup (5g) chopped parsley
Pinch of salt
Pinch of pepper

Trim any visible fat from the chicken breasts, and with a boning knife, slice each breast sideways almost all the way through. With plastic wrap underneath and on top, pound each breast with a meat mallet to about a ¼-inch (6-mm) thickness, being careful not to tear the meat. In a medium bowl, mix all the marinade ingredients together.

Place the chicken flats and the marinade mixture in a resealable plastic freezer bag, massage well and refrigerate for 4 hours or overnight, massaging occasionally.

To make the stuffing, heat the oil in a fry pan. When it is hot, sauté the mushrooms, shallots and minced garlic until soft but not browned. Set aside to cool. In a small bowl, combine the cream cheese with the Parmesan cheese, parsley, salt and pepper until well mixed. Set aside.

Set the Egg for 350°F (177°C) indirect with a drip pan. With the top and bottom vents wide open, light the fire and close the Egg. When the dome temperature gets up to about 250°F (121°C), about 10 minutes, close the bottom screen. When the dome temperature approaches 350°F (177°C), about 5-10 minutes, slide the top of the daisy wheel partially closed, leaving it ¼ of the way open.

Remove the chicken from the marinade. Lay each piece flat on a piece of plastic wrap. Spread one quarter of the cheese stuffing mixture on each breast. Roll each breast into a roll, starting on the side nearest you. Lift the plastic wrap nearest you to get started. Tie the roll with butcher's twine every inch (2.5cm), or use long toothpicks to maintain the roll shape.

Coat each roll with olive oil and add salt and pepper or your favorite rub. Place on the Egg and grill, dome closed, turning a few times, until the internal temperature reaches 165°F (74°C), about 15 minutes. Let rest under tented aluminum foil on a rack for about 5 minutes. Remove the butcher's twine or toothpicks and serve.

SLOW-ROASTED COUNTRY-STYLE PORK RIBS

Around here, "country-style" pork ribs are not ribs at all. They are either cut from the loin area (less red, more pink and white) or from the shoulder area (more red, less pink, more fat). I greatly prefer the "ribs" cut from the shoulder. They are more flavorful and less dry than "ribs" cut from the loin. You can cook them for less time at a higher temperature, but I find that a slower cook time is well worth the wait. If you don't see them in the meat case, ask your butcher to slice a pork butt into 1-inch to 1½- inch (2.5-cm to 4-cm) thick "ribs."

MAKES 8 SERVINGS

8 "country-style" pork ribs

2 tablespoons (30ml) yellow mustard (vegetable oil can be substituted if you prefer)

½ cup (60g) Pork Rub (page 208)

Maple or applewood chunks

Barbecue sauce, if desired

Trim any fat off the meat, leaving no more than ¼ inch (6mm). Cut off any sinew or cartilage and check for bone chips. Pat the meat dry and add mustard or oil. Coat all sides of the meat with rub.

Set the Egg for 250°F (121°C) indirect with a drip pan. With the top and bottom vents wide open, light the fire and close the Egg. When the dome temperature gets up to about 200°F (93°C), about 10 minutes, close the bottom screen. When the dome temperature approaches 250°F (121°C), about 5 minutes, slide the top of the daisy wheel closed, leaving the daisy wheel petals halfway open. Add maple or applewood chunks to the hot coals.

With the dome closed, cook ribs for about 3 hours, turning occasionally. Internal temperature should be between 190°F and 200°F (88°C and 93°C). Sauce during the last 15 minutes of cooking time, if desired.

SPICY CHICKEN WINGS

Chicken wings are my favorite white meat part of the chicken. If they are properly cooked, I enjoy them grilled, smoked or deep-fried. Like most Eggheads, I prefer dry wings over wet. I find that, too often, the sauce covers up the crispy flavors in the meat's surface. This recipe, however, accents the spicy, dry rub on the wings with a sweet, spicy and savory glaze.

MAKES ABOUT 8 SERVINGS

2 pounds (1kg) whole chicken wings, tips removed

½ cup (120ml) olive oil

SPICE RUB

1 tablespoon (15g) salt

¼ cup (50g) brown sugar

1 teaspoon (2g) black pepper

2 tablespoons (14g) paprika

1 teaspoon (2g) cayenne pepper

¼ cup (32g) ancho chili powder

GLAZE

4 ounces (113g) unsalted butter

2 tablespoons (30ml) apple cider vinegar

1 cup (237ml) honey

¼ cup (59ml) Dijon mustard

1 tablespoon (7g) chili powder

1 teaspoon (6g) salt

In a medium bowl, mix all the spice rub ingredients together. Rub the wings with olive oil, then rub with the spice mixture and set aside.

Set the Egg for 350°F (177°C) indirect with a drip pan. With the top and bottom vents wide open, light the fire and close the Egg. When the dome temperature gets up to about 250°F (121°C), about 10 minutes, close the bottom screen. When the dome temperature approaches 350°F (177°C), about 5-10 minutes, slide the top of the daisy wheel partially closed, leaving it ¼ of the way open.

For the glaze, melt the butter in a medium saucepan over medium heat. Add the vinegar, honey and mustard and blend well. Add the chili powder and salt, mix well and remove from the heat.

When the Egg is up to temperature, place the wings on the grid and grill, dome closed, until the internal temperature reaches 180°F (82°C), about 25 minutes. Turn the wings every five minutes to prevent burning. When the wings are cooked, dip them in the sauce and place them back on the Egg for 5 to 10 minutes to glaze up, being careful not to burn them. Remove from the Egg and wait about 10 minutes before serving.

PRIMETIME RIB ROAST

Prime rib is usually prepared for special occasions. I consider supper a special occasion. When you cook prime rib, you usually have a lot going on in the kitchen. Using the Egg not only frees up the kitchen, but gives the roast a crusty bark and smoky flavor that no oven can! It makes special occasions even more special.

MAKES ABOUT 10 SERVINGS

1 (7-pound [3kg]) standing rib roast, first cut, 3 to 4 ribs

Olive oil

½ cup (60g) Beef Rub (see page 208)

Tiger Sauce (page 39)

Trim the fat from the roast, leaving ¼ inch (6mm). Rub all over with olive oil, and then dry rub. Tie two pieces of butcher's twine around the roast between the bones. Let sit at room temperature for 1 hour before cooking.

Set up the Egg for 350°F (177°C) indirect with a drip pan. With the top and bottom vents wide open, light the fire and close the Egg. When the dome temperature gets up to about 250°F (121°C), about 10 minutes, close the bottom screen. When the temperature approaches 350°F (177°C), about 5-10 minutes, slide the top of the daisy wheel partially closed, leaving it ¼ of the way open.

When the Egg is up to temperature, place the roast on the grid, bone side down. Close the dome and cook for 1½ to 1¾ hours, until the internal temperature reaches 125°F (52°C), rotating the meat every 15 minutes. When it is cooked, remove from the Egg and tent under aluminum foil on a rack to rest for 20 minutes. The temperature will rise another 10°F (5°C) for medium rare. If you like your roast more medium, remove it from the Egg when it reaches 135°F (57°C). Because the roast is not a uniform thickness, the thinner parts will be cooked more than the thicker parts. You can cook it to the degree of doneness that you and your guests prefer.

To carve, remove the twine and slice the roast away from the rib bone section, leaving the rib bones attached to each other. Place the roast cut side down and slice across the grain in ¾-inch to 1-inch (2-cm to 2.5-cm) slices. Slice the rib bones apart and give to your favorite guest, or hide them for yourself! Serve with Tiger Sauce on the side.

SPICY SHRIMP PO' BOY

Grilled shrimp taste great if they aren't cooked too long. They can easily be overcooked. When cooked right, they will have a little snap at the center and not be chewy. This marinade helps keep them moist and adds a "spicy canvas" with sweet and sour notes. The Po' Boy sandwich gives extra crunch, crispiness and creaminess to every bite. The mayonnaise in the sauce will help tame the heat. This recipe makes only four Po' Boys, so if you aren't eating alone, you'll need to make more!

MAKES 4 PO' BOYS

1 pound (454g) raw shrimp, 31 to 40 count, peeled and deveined

1 French baguette, cut into four 6-inch (15-cm) pieces

4 leaves of lettuce

2 large ripe tomatoes, sliced

Salt and pepper

SHRIMP SPICE MARINADE

1 tablespoon (15ml) olive oil

1 tablespoon (15ml) lime juice

1 teaspoon (5ml) hot sauce (I prefer Pete's)

1 tablespoon (13g) light brown sugar

1 tablespoon (15ml) honey

2 teaspoons (6g) smoked paprika

1 teaspoon (3g) onion powder

1 teaspoon (3g) garlic powder

1 teaspoon (6g) salt

1 teaspoon (2g) fresh ground pepper

½ teaspoon cayenne pepper

PO' BOY SAUCE

½ cup (120ml) mayonnaise

½ cup (120ml) ketchup

¼ cup (38g) finely chopped red onion

3 tablespoons (9g) chopped green onion

2 tablespoons (30ml) chili sauce

1 tablespoon (15ml) prepared horseradish

In a large bowl, mix the liquid marinade ingredients together, then add the remaining ingredients and mix well. Add the shrimp and let marinate for 30 to 60 minutes.

In a medium bowl, mix all of the sauce ingredients together until well combined. Slice the baguette into four equal pieces, then slice those pieces in half. Spread the sauce on both the top and bottom pieces. Lay the lettuce leaves on the bottom section and add sliced tomato to each. Salt and pepper the tomato slices.

Set the Egg for 400°F (204°C) direct on a raised grate and a perforated cooking grid. With the top and bottom vents wide open, light the fire and close the Egg. When the dome temperature gets up to about 250°F (121°C), about 10 minutes, close the bottom screen. When the dome temperature approaches 400°F (204°C), about 10 minutes, slide the top of the daisy wheel partially closed, leaving it ¼ of the way open.

When the Egg is up to temperature, lay the shrimp on the grate, cook for 3 minutes, flip and cook for an additional 2 minutes. The shrimp should be pink. Do not leave them on the heat too long or they will get overcooked. They should have a little give and will be moist with a little crunch. When overcooked, they are more white, dense and chewy. Remove the shrimp to a plate, divide them among the four Po' Boys and cover with the top of the baguette to serve.

CEDAR-PLANKED SALMON

I have fished for salmon in the Northeast and the Northwest. I once went cross-country with my mother's cousin Bud (my first cousin, once removed), and we stayed with his brothers Jimmy and Jerry, who are fishing guides on the Rogue River in Oregon. We fished in the drift boats but, sadly, the salmon run was over. I grew up fishing for landlocked salmon after ice-out with my father, my Uncle Howard and my cousins Mark and Matt. We fished New Hampshire's Lake Winnepesaukee and Newfound Lake. The fishing was great, but the recipe for Cedar Planked Salmon is the best I've ever eaten! Northwest Indians cooked salmon on cedar planks long before the Europeans came to America. The cedar gives a pleasant smoky flavor to the fish, which is rich and buttery. The key to moist salmon fillets is to cook to no more than medium-rare. The glaze is sweet and tangy, with a little heat on the back end. You will never buy canned salmon again!

MAKES ABOUT 6 SERVINGS

2 pound (900g) salmon fillets, skin on

2 cedar planks

½ cup (100g) brown sugar

2 tablespoons (30ml) Dijon mustard

1 teaspoon (2g) cayenne pepper

1 tablespoon (15ml) lemon juice

2 tablespoons (30ml) olive oil

1 teaspoon (6g) salt

1 teaspoon (2g) fresh ground black pepper

Soak the cedar planks in water for 2 hours prior to the cook.

Set the Egg for 400°F (204°C) direct. With the top and bottom vents wide open, light the fire and close the Egg. When the dome temperature gets up to about 250°F (121°C), about 10 minutes, close the bottom screen. When the dome temperature approaches 400°F (204°C), about 10 minutes, slide the top of the daisy wheel partially closed, leaving it ¼ of the way open.

In a small bowl, combine the brown sugar, mustard, cayenne and lemon juice until well mixed. Wash the salmon in cold water and pat dry. Brush your fingertips along the flesh of the fillet to check for bones. Rub both sides of the fillet with oil and sprinkle with salt and pepper. When the Egg is up to temperature, place the soaked planks on the grid until they start to smoke, about 3 minutes, then flip over. Place the fillets on the planks, skin side down. Spread the sauce on the top of the fillet, close the dome and cook until the internal temperature in the thickest part reaches 135°F (57°C), about 10 minutes. Have a spray bottle available with water or apple cider to spray on any flare-ups. Remove fillets from the Egg and let rest under tented aluminum foil for 5 minutes.

GRILL-ROASTED BEEF SHORT RIBS

Next to brisket point, beef short ribs are the best part of the cow, pound for pound, for tenderness and beefy flavor. They must be cooked for a long time to become tender. Most recipes braise the ribs. Braising does tenderize, but the beef picks up much of the braising liquid's flavors and much of the beef flavor is lost, with little smoke flavor added. This recipe smokes them like a brisket and wraps them in foil with just a little liquid to complete the cook and make them very tender. The beefy flavor is very present, with a little smoke and braising liquid flavor. I have not sauced because I think the sauce hides the great beef taste. If you prefer, serve sauce on the side.

MAKES ABOUT 6 SERVINGS

10 beef short ribs cut into individual bones

¼ cup (60ml) olive oil

½ cup (50g) Beef Rub (page 208)

1 chunk pecan wood

1 pint (500ml) Rick's Sinful Marinade (page 30)

Coat each rib with olive oil, then rub with the beef rub.

Set the Egg for 250°F (121°C) indirect with a drip pan. With the top and bottom vents wide open, light the fire and close the Egg. When the dome temperature gets up to about 200°F (93°C), about 10 minutes, close the bottom screen. When the dome temperature approaches 250°F (121°C), about 5 minutes, slide the top of the daisy wheel closed, keeping the daisy wheel petals halfway open.

When the Egg is up to temperature, add the chunk of pecan to the charcoal. After the smoke has died down to a bluish-gray color, put the ribs on the grid, bone-side down and at least ¼ inch (6mm) apart and close the dome. Rotate the ribs after one hour. When the internal temperature reaches 160°F (71°C)—about two hours—remove the ribs from the fire. Set the ribs on top of a double layer of aluminum foil, 3 or 4 bones to a packet, meat-side down, and wrap tightly. Before closing one end, add Rick's Sinful Marinade. Place back on the Egg until the internal temperature reaches 200°F (93°C), about one hour. When cooked, remove the foil packets from the Egg and let them rest for 10 minutes. After the resting period, remove the ribs from the foil and serve, bone-side down, reserving the marinade in the foil for dipping.

TEQUILA LIME CHICKEN THIGHS

Did I have you at "tequila"? The thighs are the juiciest part of the chicken, and when cooked to 165°F (74°C), they are both tender and juicy. The tequila marinade infuses a flavor on and into the chicken to make you want more, bite after bite. *Muy bien!*

MAKES ABOUT 8 SERVINGS

8 chicken thighs, bone in, skin off

¼ cup (60ml) good-quality tequila, 100% agave

2 tablespoons (19g) minced garlic

1 jalapeño pepper, diced

2 tablespoons (30ml) lime juice

¼ cup (60ml) orange juice

½ teaspoon salt

½ teaspoon black pepper

1 tablespoon (2.5g) finely chopped fresh cilantro

1 tablespoon (15ml) olive oil

Whisk together all ingredients except the chicken in a medium-sized bowl. Place the marinade in a resealable plastic freezer bag and add the skinless thighs. Massage the marinade around the chicken. Lay bag flat in a baking dish and refrigerate for 4 to 6 hours, turning occasionally.

Set the Egg for 350°F (177°C) indirect with a drip pan. With the top and bottom vents wide open, light the fire and close the Egg. When the dome temperature gets up to about 250°F (121°C), about 10 minutes, close the bottom screen. When the dome temperature approaches 350°F (177°C), about 5-10 minutes, slide the top of the daisy wheel partially closed, leaving it ¼ of the way open.

When the Egg is up to temperature, remove the chicken from the marinade and place on the grate and close the dome. Discard the marinade.

Grill the chicken until it reaches an internal temperature of 165°F (74°C), about 25 minutes. Remove from the Egg and set on a rack, tented with aluminum foil, for 10 minutes before serving.

BOURBON MOXIE™ MEATBALLS

In my drinkin' days, bourbon was my favorite, and Moxie™ still is. Moxie™ is a soda from Maine that's been around since 1876. It was originally advertised to cure everything from paralysis and nervousness to softening of the brain! It is an acquired taste, great for sipping, not so much for chugging. I suppose it's a lot like bourbon that way. These meatballs have the softer texture of a meatloaf, as opposed to a firm meatball. With the charcoal fire, they pick up a hint of smoke. Life is good!

MAKES ABOUT 4 SERVINGS

2 tablespoons (30g) unsalted butter

¼ cup (38g) finely chopped onion

1 clove garlic, minced

¼ cup (40g) finely chopped celery

¼ cup (19g) chopped mushrooms

3 slices bacon, diced

1 pound (454g) 80/20 ground chuck

¼ cup (15g) fresh breadcrumbs

1 large egg, lightly beaten

1 tablespoon (15ml) bourbon

1 tablespoon (15ml) Moxie™

1 teaspoon (5ml) Worcestershire sauce

½ teaspoon kosher salt

¼ teaspoon black pepper

Beef Rub (page 208)

Melt the butter in a saucepan; add onion, garlic and celery and sauté for 3 to 4 minutes, until softened but not browned. Add mushrooms and diced bacon and continue to cook until soft, another 4 minutes. Remove from heat and cool in a large mixing bowl.

When the vegetables have cooled, add the beef, breadcrumbs, egg, bourbon, Moxie™, Worcestershire sauce, salt and pepper to the bowl and mix all the ingredients together. Mix thoroughly, but don't over-squeeze the meat, because it makes the meatballs drier and more dense. Gently roll the mixture into 1-inch (2.5-cm) meatballs and apply the rub.

Set the Egg for 350°F (177°C) indirect with a drip pan. With the top and bottom vents wide open, light the fire and close the Egg. When the dome temperature gets up to about 250°F (121°C), about 10 minutes, close the bottom screen. When the dome temperature approaches 350°F (177°C), about 5-10 minutes, slide the top of the daisy wheel partially closed, leaving it ¼ of the way open.

Close the dome and roast the meatballs, turning once halfway through, for approximately 20 minutes, or to an internal temperature of 160°F (71°C). Serve with toothpicks.

GARLIC SAUSAGE FATTIES

A fattie is not much more in size and appearance than a one-pound Jimmy Dean™ sausage roll. Rub is placed on it and it is roasted. You can experiment with other kinds of sausage, and the fatties can be stuffed or even wrapped in bacon. Add sauce if you'd like. As a variation, the raw sausage can be rolled into 1-inch (2.5-cm) round sausage balls, covered in rub and cooked indirectly over a drip pan at 350°F (177°C) for 15 to 20 minutes, to an internal temperature of 160°F (71°C).

MAKES ABOUT 12 SERVINGS

3 pounds (1350g) pork shoulder, bone removed

½ pound (225g) thick-cut, hickory-smoked bacon

2 tablespoons (19g) minced garlic

½ cup (45g) chopped green and red jalapeños, seeds and ribs removed

1 tablespoon (13g) turbinado sugar

¾ teaspoon nutmeg

½ teaspoon allspice

¾ tablespoon (6g) crushed black pepper

½ teaspoon cayenne pepper

⅓ cup (78ml) chicken broth

Pork Rub (page 208)

Cut the pork shoulder into 1 by 1-inch (2.5 by 2.5-cm) strips, removing silver skin and cartilage. Using a coarse grind plate, grind the pork a few pieces at a time, then grind a slice of bacon. Alternate grinding several pieces of pork with a slice of bacon to get a good mix.

In a large bowl, add the remainder of the ingredients, except the pork rub, and mix gently by hand with half of the ground meat. You can tell that the spices and peppers are mixed in well when they look uniform in the bowl. Don't over-squeeze the meat, as it will make the sausage drier. Add the remainder of the ground meat to the bowl and gently mix.

Form the finished sausage into 3 one-pound (450-g) logs, about 2 inches (5cm) in diameter. Place one log at the end of a long piece of plastic wrap and begin to roll, keeping the log tight as you roll. When complete, there should be no air pockets and the roll should be firm to the touch. Roll the remaining two logs. Refrigerate for half an hour. If not using all sausage, place the remainder in a resealable bag and freeze for later use.

Set the Egg for 350°F (177°C) indirect with a drip pan. With the top and bottom vents wide open, light the fire and close the Egg. When the dome temperature gets up to about 250°F (121°C), about 10 minutes, close the bottom screen. When the dome temperature approaches 350°F (177°C), about 5-10 minutes, slide the top of the daisy wheel partially closed, leaving it ¼ of the way open.

Remove the log, now a fattie, from the plastic wrap and coat it liberally with pork rub. Place the fattie on the Egg, close the dome and cook for 30 minutes until the internal temperature reaches 160°F (71°C). Remove from heat, tent with foil and let rest for 10 minutes before slicing into ½-inch (1.5-cm) slices.

APPLE PIE PORK LOIN

Pork loin is a nice chunk of meat, but it is lean and not very flavorful. Brining helps keep the pork moist and adds a little flavor. My Uncle Donald told me that a piece of apple pie isn't right unless you add cheddar cheese to it. I learned at an early age that apple pie and cheese go together, and I know that apples and pork go together, so there you have it!

MAKES ABOUT 16 SERVINGS

1 (4-pound [1814g]) boneless pork loin, from blade end if possible

1 (16-ounce [454g]) can of apple pie filling

½ cup (60g) shredded cheddar cheese

2 tablespoons (30ml) olive oil

¼ cup (30g) Pork Rub (page 208)

BRINE

¾ cup (150g) granulated sugar

6 tablespoons (108g) table salt

8 cups (2L) water, divided

2 tablespoons (19g) minced garlic

2 tablespoons (20g) black peppercorns

Cut into the roast ½ inch (1.5cm) deep along its length and continue to cut in a circular or spiral pattern so the roast evenly lies flat, and is about ½ inch (1.5cm) thick. Place the flattened meat between two sheets of plastic wrap and smooth it out by pounding with a meat mallet to about a ⅜-inch (9-mm) thickness.

Mix the salt and sugar in a large microwavable dish with 2 cups (473ml) of water. Microwave until the salt and sugar dissolve. Add the remaining 6 cups (1.4L) of water, the garlic and the peppercorns and stir to combine. Place the flattened loin in the brine and refrigerate for 1 hour.

Set up the Egg for 375°F (191°C) indirect with a drip pan. With the top and bottom vents wide open, light the fire and close the Egg. When the dome temperature gets up to about 250°F (121°C), about 10 minutes, close the bottom screen. When the dome temperature approaches 375°F (191°C), about 5-10 minutes, slide the top of the daisy wheel partially closed, leaving it ¼ of the way open.

After the loin has brined for 1 hour, remove from the brine, rinse off with water and pat it dry. Place the flattened loin on 3 sheets of plastic wrap. Spread the pie filling all over the loin. Spread the cheese uniformly onto the pie filling. Starting at the end nearest you, roll the flattened loin up like a jellyroll. Tie the roll every 1 inch (2.5cm) with wet butcher's twine. Coat the roll with olive oil and rub it with pork rub.

When the Egg is up to temperature, place the roll on the grid, close the dome, and cook until the internal temperature is 145°F (63°C), turning 3 times, for about an hour. When cooked, remove the roast from the Egg and place it under tented aluminum foil on a rack. When it has rested for 10 minutes, slice into ½-inch (1.5-cm) slices, removing the butcher's twine as you slice.

MISO MANGO FISH TACOS

This recipe can be used with any white fish. The Japanese-flavored marinade will firm the fish a little as it does its thing, and when the fish is grilled, there will be a little char from the sugars in the marinade. The sweetness of the mango in the slaw brings out the sweetness of the fish. The crunch and creaminess of the slaw makes every bite of this taco a fish-eater's delight. The miso marinade can also be reduced and used as a glaze on grilled fish, chicken, vegetables or tofu.

MAKES 6 SERVINGS

2 pounds (900g) haddock or cod fillets

12 (6-inch [15cm]) soft flour tortillas

MISO MARINADE

½ cup (56g) white miso paste

½ cup (120ml) sake or mirin

⅓ cup (63g) white sugar

1 tablespoon (10g) minced ginger

1 teaspoon (5ml) rice wine vinegar

MANGO SLAW

1 mango, peeled and thinly sliced

¼ cup (60ml) mayonnaise

1 tablespoon (15ml) lime juice

¼ teaspoon salt

Pinch of pepper

1 (8 ounce [227g]) bag of cabbage slaw mix with carrots

½ cup (76g) red onion, sliced thinly

¼ cup (4g) chopped fresh cilantro

In a medium bowl, whisk the marinade ingredients together until the miso and sugar are well combined with the liquid. Cut the fillets into ¾-inch (2cm) thick slices and place them in a resealable plastic freezer bag with the marinade. Refrigerate for 6 to 12 hours.

To make the slaw, mix the mayonnaise, lime juice, salt and pepper in a small bowl until well blended. In a separate medium bowl, toss the cabbage, onion and cilantro together, then add the mayonnaise mixture and mix well to combine. Add the mango slices and toss lightly.

Set up the Egg for 350°F (177°C) indirect with a drip pan. With the top and bottom vents wide open, light the fire and close the Egg. When the dome temperature gets up to about 250°F (121°C), about 10 minutes, close the bottom screen. When the dome temperature approaches 350°F (177°C), about 5-10 minutes, slide the top of the daisy wheel partially closed, leaving it ¼ of the way open.

When the Egg is up to temperature, grill the fish with the dome closed for about 4 minutes. Flip and cook for another 3 minutes, until the internal temperature reaches about 135°F (57°C). Remove from the Egg and place under an aluminum foil tent on a rack to rest for 5 minutes.

Make 6 piles of 2 taco shells each and divide the fish and mango slaw among them, then serve.

TENDER ROASTED RACK OF LAMB

Lamb is very popular in other parts of the world, but historically not so much in the United States. Nowadays, rack of lamb is available in most large supermarkets and wholesale clubs. It grills extremely well, giving a crispy outside and a tender, medium-rare inside.

MAKES ABOUT 6 SERVINGS

2 racks of lamb, about 1½ pounds (675g) each

2 tablespoons (30ml) olive oil

2 tablespoons (2g) finely chopped fresh rosemary

2 teaspoons (10g) kosher salt

Pepper

Trim any visible fat from the racks. One end may be thicker than the other because racks have a layer of fat with a thin layer of meat beneath, and another layer of fat under the thin layer of meat. Remove both layers of fat and any silver skin. French the bone tips by cutting off any fat, meat or tissues. Rub the racks with olive oil, then with the rosemary, salt and pepper.

Set the Egg for 350°F (177°C) indirect with a drip pan. With the top and bottom vents wide open, light the fire and close the Egg. When the dome temperature gets up to about 250°F (121°C), about 10 minutes, close the bottom screen. When the dome temperature approaches 350°F (177°C), about 5-10 minutes, slide the top of the daisy wheel partially closed, leaving it ¼ of the way open.

When the Egg is up to temperature, place the lamb racks on the grid, bone side down. Cook, dome closed, for 25 to 30 minutes, until the internal temperature in the thickest part reaches 125°F (52°C) for medium-rare, rotating the meat every 10 minutes. When cooked, remove from the Egg and tent on a rack under aluminum foil for 10 minutes. Slice between the bones and serve.

ROASTED BONELESS TURKEY BREAST

When you are expecting a large gathering, like at Thanksgiving, smoking a whole, fresh, all-natural turkey that you have brined yourself is the best way to go. However, when you just want moist, flavorful turkey breast, roasting a frozen, boneless, skin-on, enhanced breast is very easy and good. The enhanced breasts are injected with a flavored saline solution by the provider. I know the grill gods are convening as I speak, but this recipe really is very good! Obviously, you can buy a fresh, un-enhanced boneless breast and brine it yourself, but trust me, you won't be sorry. In fact, while you are at it, why not make two?

MAKES ABOUT 8 SERVINGS

1 (3-pound [1361g]) fresh or frozen boneless turkey breast, injected with saline solution

2 tablespoons (30ml) olive oil

¼ cup (30g) Chicken Rub (page 209)

Set up the Egg for 350°F (177°C) indirect with a drip pan. With the top and bottom vents wide open, light the fire and close the Egg. When the dome temperature gets up to about 250°F (121°C), about 10 minutes, close the bottom screen. When the dome temperature approaches 350°F (177°C), about 5-10 minutes, slide the top of the daisy wheel partially closed, leaving it ¼ of the way open.

Rinse the thawed turkey breast with cold water and pat dry. Rub all over with olive oil, then rub with the chicken rub, under and on top of the skin. Roll the breast into a small football to help it cook more evenly.

When the Egg is up to temperature, roast the turkey breast, dome closed, until the internal temperature reaches 165°F (74°C), about 60 minutes. When cooled, remove the breast and tent with aluminum foil on a rack for 10 minutes before slicing and serving.

TENDER TURKEY TENDERLOIN WITH RASPBERRY-LIME GLAZE

One day, I was going through the supermarket to pick up a few last-minute items for NewEgglandfest VII in Brentwood, New Hampshire. In the meat display, between the beef steaks, were turkey tenderloins. I decided these would be great to serve at NewEgglandfest. I used raspberry glaze, and those tenderloins were a huge hit! They were moist, tender, sweet and a little spicy. You won't be disappointed! I prefer seeds in my jam. If you don't, try seedless or other fruit jams or jellies.

MAKES ABOUT 6 SERVINGS

4 turkey breast tenderloins

2 tablespoons (30ml) olive oil

4 tablespoons (30g) Chicken Rub (page 209)

½ cup (120ml) raspberry jam

2 tablespoons (30ml) lime juice

1 tablespoon (14g) unsalted butter

1 tablespoon (10g) minced jalapeño pepper, ribs and seeds removed

¼ teaspoon salt

Set up the Egg for 350°F (177°C) indirect with a drip pan. With the top and bottom vents wide open, light the fire and close the Egg. When the dome temperature gets up to about 250°F (121°C), about 10 minutes, close the bottom screen. When the dome temperature approaches 350°F (177°C), about 5-10 minutes, slide the top of the daisy wheel partially closed, leaving it ¼ of the way open.

Cut any visible fat off the tenderloins, rinse in water and pat dry. Coat each tenderloin with olive oil, then rub 1 tablespoon (7g) rub to each piece.

In a sauce pan, over low heat, slowly combine the jam, lime juice and butter. Add the jalapeño pepper and salt, continuing to stir and heat until well blended. Sauce should not be runny.

When the Egg is up to temperature, place the turkey on the oiled grid, close the dome, and cook until the internal temperature reaches 160°F (71°C), about 15 minutes, turning and flipping a few times. Brush the raspberry lime sauce on all sides and let glaze 5 to 10 more minutes, or until the internal temperature reaches 165°F (74°C). Remove from the Egg and let rest under tented aluminum foil on a rack for 10 minutes. If you prefer, double the raspberry lime sauce and reserve one half for serving.

SEAFOOD PAELLA

Paella has its roots in Spain and is a great way to cook and serve fresh seafood family style. One of the keys is cooking the rice to form a little crust in the bottom of the pan when ready to serve. During the cook, the chorizo cooks down and creates a miraculous, spicy gravy that all of the ingredients bathe in. Great additions or substitutions are boneless chicken thighs, scallops and pork loin. Great served with warm bread!

MAKES 8 TO 12 SERVINGS

¼ cup (60ml) olive oil

½ cup (76g) onions

2 tablespoons (19g) chopped garlic

½ cup (76g) red bell peppers, seeded and chopped

1 pound (454g) shrimp, shell on, 16 to 20 count

½ pound (224g) chorizo, diced in ½-inch (1.5-cm) pieces

2 teaspoons (6g) smoked paprika

1½ cups (316g) uncooked Arborio rice

6 to 8 cups (1.4–1.9L) low-sodium chicken broth, divided

1 teaspoon (1g) saffron

½ cup (76g) chopped tomatoes

½ teaspoon thyme

1 teaspoon (6g) salt

1 teaspoon (2g) black pepper

1 pound (454g) white fish fillet, cut into 1-inch (2.5-cm) cubes

½ pound (225g) clams, scrubbed clean under cold water

1 tablespoon (2.5g) chopped flat-leaf parsley

8 lemon wedges

Set the Egg for 350°F (177°C) direct. With the top and bottom vents wide open, light the fire and close the Egg. When the dome temperature gets up to about 250°F (121°C), about 10 minutes, close the bottom screen. When the dome temperature approaches 350°F (177°C), about 5-10 minutes, slide the top of the daisy wheel partially closed, leaving it ¼ of the way open.

In a Dutch oven or cast iron 10-inch (22-cm) skillet or paella pan, heat the olive oil. Sauté the onions, garlic and bell peppers until soft but not browned, about 5 minutes. Add the chorizo and paprika and continue to sauté 5 minutes more. Add the rice and sauté until the rice is lightly browned, about 5 minutes more. Add 3 cups (700ml) of the chicken broth, saffron and tomatoes and cover to bring to a boil. Close the dome and simmer for 15 to 20 minutes, until the rice is still slightly firm. Add more chicken broth as necessary to keep the rice cooking. If you run out of broth before the rice cooks to slightly firm, add a cup (237ml) of water. Add the thyme, salt and black pepper. Place the raw shrimp and the clams on top of the pan and push down slightly into the rice mixture. Cover and cook for another 10 minutes, until the shrimp are pink and the clams have opened. Remove from the heat and sprinkle the parsley on top. Let rest about 5 minutes, discarding any unopened clams. Serve with lemon wedges.

BARBECUED BOLOGNA

I first had barbecued bologna at my Uncle Sid and Aunt Mac's farm during a family reunion. Uncle Sid cooked it on a rotisserie oven grill. It did taste good! I didn't know whether barbecuing bologna was Sid's way of being frugal or his way showing us that simple and cheap can be better than elaborate and expensive. Roasting on the Egg makes the smoke flavor penetrate the meat. I choose to cook it dry, with rub only, instead of wet with sauce applied before finishing. A variation would be to try another chunk of meat, such as olive loaf. Your butcher at the market would be happy to cut you a hunk. Tell him what you are cooking, and he'll be licking his chops!

MAKES ABOUT 12 SERVINGS

1 (4-pound chunk [1800g]) whole bologna
2 tablespoons (30ml) mustard or vegetable oil
¼ cup (30g) Beef Rub (page 208)
Barbecue sauce for serving

Remove the bologna from its plastic wrapper and pat dry. Slice a diamond pattern about ½ inch (1.5cm) deep and 1 inch (2.5cm) apart all around the bologna. Rub the scored bologna with either the yellow mustard or the vegetable oil and apply the dry rub.

Set the Egg for 225°F (107°C) indirect cook. With the top and bottom vents wide open, light the fire and close the Egg. When the dome temperature gets up to about 200°F (93°C), about 5-10 minutes, close the bottom screen. When the dome temperature approaches 225°F (107°C), about 5 minutes, slide the top of the daisy wheel closed, leaving the daisy wheel petals ¼ of the way open.

Place the rubbed bologna on a rack with the drip pan underneath. Roast for 3 to 4 hours, turning occasionally, with the dome closed. There should be a nice bark on the outside when it's finished.

When done, remove from the fire and let it rest for 10 minutes before slicing. Serve your favorite barbecue sauce on the side.

ABT: A BEAUTIFUL THING

"ABT" is short for "Atomic Buffalo Turds," a recipe that has been around for many years. ABTs are sliced jalapeño peppers filled with pulled pork and wrapped in bacon. They are spicy and don't look very appealing when finished, but the taste is fantastic! Variations are numerous. I renamed them for mixed company.

MAKES 12 ABTS

6 jalapeño peppers
4 ounces (120g) cream cheese
2 ripe nectarines
6 slices regular-cut bacon
Rub of choice

Slice the jalapeño peppers lengthwise. Using the tip of a rounded teaspoon, scrape the seeds and ribs out of the peppers. These have the most heat. If you prefer, you can leave the ribs in, but they will be HOT! Using a spoon or a table knife, spread cream cheese into each pepper half, leveling to the cut sides. Slice the nectarines into 6 slices each, and place one slice in each pepper half with the skin side facing up. Cut each bacon slice in half and wrap it completely around the filled pepper half, overlapping if necessary. Sprinkle rub on each ABT.

Set the Egg for 350°F (177°C) indirect with a drip pan. With the top and bottom vents wide open, light the fire and close the Egg. When the dome temperature gets up to about 250°F (121°C), about 10 minutes, close the bottom screen. When the dome temperature approaches 350°F (177°C), about 5-10 minutes, slide the top of the daisy wheel partially closed, leaving it ¼ of the way open.

Place the ABTs on the grid, close the dome and cook until the bacon starts to crisp, about 20 minutes. When finished, remove from the fire and let rest 5 minutes before eating, so the filling won't burn your mouth!

CINDI'S BACON-WRAPPED DRIED APRICOTS WITH CRANBERRY GLAZE

Anything is good wrapped in bacon, right? Well, wait until you sink your teeth into one of these! This appetizer is a fun way to get your daily intake of bacon. It's a real crowd pleaser, with a sweet cranberry glaze covering the saltiness of the bacon. If you feel adventurous and have extra time on your hands, inject a bit of Grand Marnier into the apricots before they hit the Egg. These apricots don't last long, so make sure to sneak a few for yourself.

MAKES ABOUT 4 SERVINGS

1 pound (454g) thin-sliced bacon

1 (12-oz [.35-L]) can frozen cranberry juice cocktail concentrate

⅓ cup (66g) brown sugar

1 tablespoon (8g) favorite barbecue rub (I like Dizzy Pig™ Pineapple Head rub)

1 tablespoon (9g) cornstarch, mixed with 1 cup (240ml) water

1 pound (450g) dried apricots

The cranberry glaze works best at room temperature, so make it first. Place the cranberry juice concentrate, brown sugar and rub in a small saucepan and simmer until the sugar dissolves. Add the cornstarch mixed with water to the sauce and stir gently for 2 to 3 minutes, to desired consistency.

Set the Egg to 350°F (177°C) indirect with a drip pan. With the top and bottom vents wide open, light the fire and close the Egg. When the dome temperature gets up to about 250°F (121°C), about 10 minutes, close the bottom screen. When the dome temperature approaches 350°F (177°C), about 5-10 minutes, slide the top of the daisy wheel partially closed, leaving it ¼ of the way open.

While the Egg is heating, cut the bacon strips into thirds. Wrap each bacon strip around an apricot, securing with a toothpick. Repeat until you have no bacon left.

Close the dome and cook until the bacon is done to your liking, 10 to 20 minutes. Remove from the Egg and drizzle with the cranberry glaze while still warm.

FIRST PLACE ARMADILLO RATS

Sausage-wrapped ABTs are sometimes referred to as Armadillo Eggs. This variation uses garlic sausage for the wrap. They end up looking like rats. These don't taste all that bad, for rat!

MAKES 10 RATS

2 pounds (900g) Garlic Sausage (page 74)

10 ABTs (page 87)

Pork Rub (page 208)

Prepare and cook 10 ABTs per the recipe, with one exception. When you cut the jalapeños lengthwise, leave the stem on, and facing up. The other half can be used for an ABT, but just not for the Rats. Wrap the cooked ABTs with sausage, with the stem "tail" facing up. For added fun, cut small triangles of the nectarine skin and press them into the Rat's face for eyes! Rub the rats with pork rub.

Set the Egg for 350°F (177°C) indirect with a drip pan. With the top and bottom vents wide open, light the fire and close the Egg. When the dome temperature gets up to about 250°F (121°C), about 10 minutes, close the bottom screen. When the dome temperature approaches 350°F (177°C), about 5-10 minutes, slide the top of the daisy wheel partially closed, leaving it ¼ of the way open.

Place the meat on the grid, close the dome and cook for ½ hour until the sausage reaches an internal temperature of 160°F (71°C). Remove from the fire and let rest for 5 to 10 minutes. When ready, show the Rat who's boss and bite its head off!

FRITACOS FANTÁSTICOS

These are scoop-shaped corn chips stuffed with taco-seasoned hamburger. They grill up with a little smoke flavor, a crunch of the corn chips and a moist, spicy bite of taco meat. Once your guests get a taste of these gems, they will try to gobble them up before you get the toppings on them! Try using cheddar-jalapeño sour cream for an added kick.

MAKES ABOUT 12 SERVINGS

¼ teaspoon garlic powder

¼ teaspoon onion powder

¼ teaspoon dried oregano

½ teaspoon smoked paprika

1½ teaspoons (7g) ground cumin

1 teaspoon sea salt

½ teaspoon cayenne pepper

1 tablespoon (8g) chili powder

1 pound (454g) 93% lean ground beef

1 cup (120g) shredded cheddar cheese

¼ cup (38g) finely diced onion

¼ cup (60ml) taco sauce

1 to 2 bags scoop-shaped corn chips (I like Frito Scoops™)

8 ounces (227ml) sour cream

The beef mixture can be made ahead of time and refrigerated, but don't stuff the corn chips more than one hour before you plan to cook them, or they might get soggy.

Set the Egg for indirect heat at 350°F (177°C). With the top and bottom vents wide open, light the fire and close the Egg. When the dome temperature gets up to about 250°F (121°C), about 10 minutes, close the bottom screen. When the dome temperature approaches 350°F (177°C), about 5-10 minutes, slide the top of the daisy wheel partially closed, leaving it ¼ of the way open.

While the Egg heats, mix all of the ingredients down through the taco sauce by hand or in the large bowl of a stand mixer. Stuff a small amount of the beef mixture onto each corn chip and place on a grilling sheet for easy removal when done. Cook, dome closed, until the internal temperature reaches 160° (71°C), about 15 minutes. Remove grilling sheet.

Empty the sour cream into a resealable bag and trim ¼ inch (6mm) from the corner off the bag. When fritacos are cool enough to handle, pipe a small dollop of sour cream on each one before serving.

BIG GREEN EGGPLANT PARMIGIANA

This recipe combines the ingredients of eggplant parmigiana in a smoky, grilled version. This is a great way to enjoy the traditional flavors of baked eggplant parmigiana, cooked outside with just a hint of smoke. It can be used as an appetizer, side dish or main dish. If you use young eggplant, the skin won't be tough.

MAKES 16 SLICES

2 young eggplants, about 2 inches (5 cm) in diameter

¼ cup (60ml) olive oil

2 medium tomatoes, about 2 inches (5 cm) in diameter

2 tablespoons (19g) minced garlic

1 cup (100g) shredded Parmesan cheese, divided

1 cup (100g) shredded mozzarella cheese, divided

¼ cup (10 g) basil leaves

Salt

Pepper

Set up the Egg for 350°F (177°C) indirect with a drip pan. With the top and bottom vents wide open, light the fire and close the Egg. When the dome temperature gets up to about 250°F (121°C), about 10 minutes, close the bottom screen. When the dome temperature approaches 350°F (177°C), about 5-10 minutes, slide the top of the daisy wheel partially closed, leaving it ¼ of the way open.

Slice the eggplant into ½-inch (1.5-cm) slices (16 total) and rub with olive oil on both sides. Sprinkle with salt and pepper. Slice the tomatoes into ¼-inch (6-mm) slices (8 total).

When the Egg is up to temperature, place the eggplant slices on the grate, close the dome and grill for 10 minutes on one side, until they soften and partially cook. After 10 minutes, flip the eggplant and divide half of the Parmesan and mozzarella onto 8 slices of eggplant. Lay the tomato slices on top, sprinkle with salt and pepper and add the remainder of the divided cheese. Top with basil leaves. Grill for another 5 to 10 minutes, until the cheeses are melted. Remove from heat and serve.

PEPPERED PIG CANDY

Pig Candy is one of the first things I cooked on the Egg, and I still cook it often. I like the bacon cooked through and slightly firm but not crisp. When I bite into it, I taste the gooey, caramelized sugar, then the firmer texture of the smoky bacon, then a little heat on the back end from the cayenne. For a twist, add some chopped walnuts to the last side when you add the sugar and cayenne pepper. Gotta go now; need to make some Pig Candy!

MAKES ABOUT 6 SERVINGS

1 pound (454g) thick-cut, hickory-smoked bacon

½ cup (115g) light brown sugar, divided

1 teaspoon (2g) cayenne pepper, divided

Set the Egg for 325°F (163°C) indirect with a drip pan. With the top and bottom vents wide open, light the fire and close the Egg. When the dome temperature gets up to about 250°F (121°C), about 10 minutes, close the bottom screen. When the dome temperature approaches 325°F (163°C), about 5 minutes, slide the top of the daisy wheel partially closed, leaving it ¼ of the way open.

Lay the bacon on the grate, perpendicular to the slats; or, if you prefer, put a second grate on top of the first grate, perpendicular to the slats of the first grate. This helps keep the bacon from slipping through. With the bacon laid out, sprinkle half of the brown sugar on the upside and add half of the cayenne pepper. Close the dome. When the bacon is half cooked and the sugar is caramelized, about 20 minutes, flip the bacon and add the remaining sugar and cayenne pepper to the upside. Cook for an additional 15 minutes, until the second side is caramelized. Serve warm or refrigerate.

PULLED PORK EGG ROLLS

Egg rolls are a great way to use leftover pulled pork. Chop the pork into ⅜-inch (9-mm) pieces and mix with a little bit of barbecue sauce, but not too much. These baked egg rolls are crisp on the outside and crunchy and chewy on the inside. They are the best thing you will ever make with leftovers!

MAKES 8 ROLLS

8 egg roll wrappers

2 cups (459g) pulled pork, chopped and sauced

1 cup (30g) Cindi's Slaw (page 49)

Vegetable spray

Barbecue sauce for serving

Stack the egg roll wrappers in front of you like a diamond, with a corner towards you. Place ¼ cup (57g) of the chopped pork in the middle third of the top wrapper. Place ⅛ cup (8g) of the slaw on top of the pork. Wet the top corner with a little bit of water and wrap the closest corner over the pile of pork and slaw. Fold the sides inward, then roll the rest of the way, pressing the wet corner onto the roll to secure. Spray all over with vegetable spray.

Set the Egg for 400°F (204°C) indirect with a drip pan. With the top and bottom vents wide open, light the fire and close the Egg. When the dome temperature gets up to about 250°F (121°C), about 10 minutes, close the bottom screen. When the dome temperature approaches 400°F (204°C), about 10 minutes, slide the top of the daisy wheel partially closed, leaving it ¼ of the way open.

When the Egg is up to temperature, place the egg rolls on the grid, close the dome and bake for 20 to 25 minutes until crisp. Slice in half on the diagonal and serve with your favorite barbecue sauce.

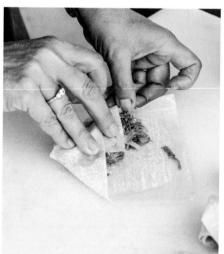

BOURBON-GLAZED CARROTS

Next to corn, carrots are my favorite vegetable. Carrots often get left off the menu when the grilling season is upon us. With the Egg, even in New Hampshire, that's year round! Boiled carrots are good, roasted are better, and bourbon-glazed are the best!

MAKES ABOUT 4 SERVINGS

1 pound (454g) baby carrots or thin carrots sliced into 2-inch (5-cm) lengths

4 tablespoons (57ml) unsalted butter

3 tablespoons (45ml) honey

1 teaspoon (3g) garlic powder

1 teaspoon (6g) salt

½ teaspoon black pepper, finely ground

3 tablespoons (45ml) bourbon

1 tablespoon (15ml) balsamic vinegar

Set the Egg for 350°F (177°C) direct. With the top and bottom vents wide open, light the fire and close the Egg. When the dome temperature gets up to about 250°F (121°C), about 10 minutes, close the bottom screen. When the dome temperature approaches 350°F (177°C), about 5-10 minutes, slide the top of the daisy wheel partially closed, leaving it ¼ of the way open.

When the Egg is up to temperature, place a Dutch oven or a cast iron pan on the grate and warm up the butter in it. Sauté the carrots for about 6 minutes, until softened, then add the honey, garlic powder, salt and pepper and sauté for another 2 minutes, until the honey is incorporated. Add the bourbon and the vinegar and sauté for another 6 minutes, until the carrots are cooked through and the liquid has reduced to a syrupy texture. Remove and serve.

GRILLED BELGIAN ENDIVE WITH BALSAMIC DRESSING

Raw endive can be bitter, but grilling it adds a different texture and smokiness. The complement of vinegar and honey gives a sweet, tart flavor, while the sugars in the honey help with caramelizing. A little crunchy, a little caramelized, a little sweet and a little tart equals a lot of texture and flavor! Grilled endive goes well with steak, chicken or anything roasted on the Egg.

MAKES 8 TO 12 SERVINGS

4 heads Belgian endive

¼ cup (60ml) olive oil

¼ cup (60ml) balsamic vinegar

1 tablespoon (9g) minced garlic

¼ cup (60ml) honey

Salt

Pepper

Set the Egg for 350°F (177°C) direct. With the top and bottom vents wide open, light the fire and close the Egg. When the dome temperature gets up to about 250°F (121°C), about 10 minutes, close the bottom screen. When the dome temperature approaches 350°F (177°C), about 5-10 minutes, slide the top of the daisy wheel partially closed, leaving it ¼ of the way open.

Prepare the endive by cutting off the root end and removing any discolored or torn leaves. Cut in half, lengthwise. In a 9 by 9-inch (22 by 22-cm) pan, mix together the olive oil, vinegar, garlic and honey. Place each endive half in the pan to coat with the mixture and sprinkle with salt and pepper. Reserve the remaining mixture.

When the Egg is up to temperature, place the endive halves, cut side down, across the grate, close the dome and cook for about 6 minutes, turning once, until the heads are tender and a little charred. Remove from the Egg and drizzle with leftover oil-vinegar mixture to serve.

GRILLED GARLIC ASPARAGUS

Asparagus is one of the first garden vegetables available in the spring. The younger spears are sweet and tender. As the season progresses, the aging spears become tougher and a little bitter. The spears are easy to grill on the Egg. With indirect cooking, they don't get overdone as you roll them back and forth. Once you've tasted these asparagus spears, you will become a fan for life.

MAKES ABOUT 8 SERVINGS

1 pound (454g) young asparagus spears, woody ends trimmed

½ cup (120ml) olive oil

½ teaspoon kosher salt

½ teaspoon ground black pepper

2 tablespoons (20g) minced garlic

1 tablespoon (15ml) lemon juice

In a small bowl, mix together the oil, salt, pepper, garlic and lemon juice. Place the mixture in a resealable plastic bag and add the asparagus, coating all the spears. Place in refrigerator for 6 to 12 hours, turning occasionally to cover asparagus.

Set the Egg for 350°F (177°C) indirect with a drip pan. With the top and bottom vents wide open, light the fire and close the Egg. When the dome temperature gets up to about 250°F (121°C), about 10 minutes, close the bottom screen. When the dome temperature approaches 350°F (177°C), about 5 minutes, slide the top of the daisy wheel partially closed, leaving it ¼ of the way open.

When the Egg is up to temperature, remove the asparagus from the bag and lay the spears across the grates. Using tongs, roll and rotate the spears for even cooking. Grill for 10 to 15 minutes until cooked but still crisp. Remove and serve.

GRILLED MEXICAN CORN ON THE COB

In my opinion, corn on the cob is like bread: fresh is best, day old is okay, but after that you luck out. At my cousin's farm in Lebanon, New Hampshire, the Patch family used to grow sweet corn on the outside rows of cow corn. We used to pick over 500 ears, dump them in the well of the Rambler station wagon and bring them home to freeze. Within 24 hours, all the kernels were off the cob and frozen. At the farm in the summer, we often ate nothing but fresh corn on the cob for dinner. This recipe calls for grilling the corn in the husk and adding a creamy, spiced spread after it is cooked. The husks keep the corn from drying out, and the smoky flavor of the grill still gets through to the crisp, juicy kernels.

MAKES 6 SERVINGS

6 ears fresh corn, husks intact

1 cup (240ml) mayonnaise

1 tablespoon (15ml) lime juice

2 tablespoons (18g) chili powder

½ teaspoon kosher salt

1 cup (122g) crumbled queso fresco or cotija cheese

For the spread, mix the mayonnaise, lime juice, chili powder and salt together. Set aside. This can be made ahead of time and refrigerated.

Set the Egg for 450°F (232°C) direct. With the top and bottom vents wide open, light the fire and close the Egg. When the dome temperature gets up to about 250°F (121°C), about 10 minutes, close the bottom screen. When the dome temperature approaches 450°F (232°C), about 10 minutes, slide the top of the daisy wheel partially closed, leaving it halfway open.

Unlike in other corn on the cob recipes, do not open the ear or remove the silk; just cut the exposed silk off the tip of the ear. It isn't necessary to soak the ears, either; just place them on the grill. Let them cook with the dome closed until the husks are charred, turning frequently, for 7 to 10 minutes. The kernels should give a little when squeezed. Remove from the Egg and let rest for 5 to 7 minutes.

Peel back the husks. The silk should release easily. Paint each ear with the spiked mayonnaise spread, sprinkle with cheese and serve.

ZUCCHINI BOATS

Zucchini and summer squash are some of the earliest summer crops. When I was a kid, I thought they tasted great, even when boiled. But as the summer months passed, our interest waned, and the squash kept growing anyway. Sometimes they reached a foot long and weighed 3 pounds (1.4kg)! Some states hold zucchini festivals to showcase what can be creatively made with overgrown zucchini. This recipe is a way to use zucchini. It ramps up the flavors with other sautéed vegetables, crumbled sausage and cheeses. The textures are both creamy and crunchy. Use your choice of sausage. For variations, you can use other ground meats, bacon, chopped tomatoes, chopped hot peppers and of course your favorite rub!

MAKES 6 BOATS

3 medium zucchini, about 8 inches (20 cm) long

½ pound (225g) sausage, removed from casing, crumbled

1 onion, chopped

2 cloves garlic, minced

1 red pepper, diced

1 teaspoon (6g) salt

1 teaspoon (2g) black pepper

1 tablespoon (15ml) lemon juice

2 tablespoons (30ml) olive oil

¼ cup (30g) dry bread crumbs

1 cup (180g) Parmesan cheese

Set the Egg to 400°F (204°C) direct. With the top and bottom vents wide open, light the fire and close the Egg. When the dome temperature gets up to about 250°F (121°C), about 10 minutes, close the bottom screen. When the dome temperature approaches 400°F (204°C), about 10 minutes, slide the top of the daisy wheel partially closed, leaving it ¼ of the way open.

In a heated cast iron pan which fits inside the Egg—including the handle—add the sausage and cook thoroughly, about 7 minutes, stirring often. Remove from the pan and add onion, garlic and red pepper. Sauté until the onions are transparent but not browned, about 5 minutes. When finished, add the sausage, salt, pepper and lemon juice and stir until well mixed. Remove from heat, drain and place in a large bowl.

Cut the zucchini in half lengthwise. With a spoon, scoop out the seeds and discard. Continue scraping the flesh until ½ inch (1.5 cm) remains. Reserve the scraped flesh, chop and set aside. Rub the scraped zucchini with olive oil and place on the Egg, cut side down, at 400°F (204°C) direct. Grill for 5 to 7 minutes, being careful not to overcook. Flip the zucchini onto the skin side and cook an additional 2 minutes.

While the zucchini is grilling, add the breadcrumbs and half of the Parmesan to the chopped zucchini flesh and mix thoroughly.

When the zucchini boat has finished grilling, remove from the heat and add the stuffing mixture to the boats, heaping above the "gunwales." Press the filling slightly to make ship shape. Sprinkle salt, pepper and remaining Parmesan cheese on top. Place the boats on the Egg at 350°F (177°C) indirect and bake, dome closed, for 10 to 15 minutes, until the Parmesan topping is lightly browned. Remove from the heat and serve.

REBECCA'S PICKLED ONIONS

This recipe is super easy and gives a nice kick to salads and sandwiches with its crunchy sweetness. It is from my daughter Rebecca. She loves pickled onions on tacos with some *barbaquoa*, grilled asparagus, queso fresco, chipotle cream sauce and fresh pea shoots. Red onions work best for the bright pink coloring, but you can use most any raw vegetable in this recipe in place of onions. Try adding different spices and herbs, or varying the amount of sugar. Agave nectar or honey can also be used in place of sugar, to desired sweetness. It's hard to go wrong, so experiment with the flavors you like!

MAKES ABOUT 6 SERVINGS

1 large red onion, halved and thinly sliced

¼ cup (60ml) red wine vinegar or apple cider vinegar

½ cup (96g) sugar

2 tablespoons (17g) whole black peppercorns

2 bay leaves

3 cloves garlic, peeled

A few sprigs fresh oregano

Kosher salt to taste

1 jalapeño pepper, thinly sliced into rings (optional)

Set a colander in the sink. Bring about 2 quarts (2L) water to a boil and pour over the onions in the colander. Let sit while you make the brine.

Add ½ cup (120ml) warm water to the vinegar in a large bowl. Stir in the sugar until dissolved. Add the peppercorns, bay leaves, garlic, oregano, salt and jalapeño (if using), then add the onions. Let stand at room temperature for at least an hour, until slightly pickled. Cover and refrigerate for up to 7 days.

BECKY'S JICAMA SALAD

My daughter Rebecca makes this version of jicama salad when she visits. If you are looking for a cool and refreshing salad to accompany most any barbecued meat, look no further! This is a basic salad, but feel free to experiment and add fruits and/or vegetables—whatever you have on hand—to make it your own!

MAKES 4 TO 6 SERVINGS

1 to 1½ pound (454 to 675g) jicama

2 or 3 carrots, peeled and thinly sliced

2 jalapeño peppers, diced, seeds and ribs removed

1 small yellow pepper, diced

¼ cup (38g) finely diced red onion

¼ cup (60ml) agave nectar

Pinch of cumin

1 teaspoon (1g) Mexican oregano

½ teaspoon (1g) smoked paprika

¼ cup (10g) chopped fresh cilantro

Peel the jicama. Using a mandolin, cut into matchsticks and place in a large bowl, adding the sliced carrots, peppers and red onion. In a separate bowl, mix the agave nectar with cumin, oregano and paprika. Pour over the chopped vegetables and let sit in the refrigerator for a couple of hours to blend the flavors. Before serving, sprinkle the chopped cilantro on top.

CHAPTER 4

THE BIG SEAR

GRILLING ON THE BIG GREEN EGG

The Big Green Egg is very well suited for grilling. As mentioned in Chapter 2, grilling is done at higher temperatures for a shorter period of time than for barbecuing. Searing temperatures on the Egg can be 450°F (230°C) and up to 750°F (399°C). This is accomplished directly, and sometimes directly to sear, then indirectly to finish (roast). The key is to create a flavorful crust on the outside while letting the inside cook to the desired doneness, which is usually medium rare for me. If you use too high a temperature, you can end up cooking the outside of the meat before the inside is done, or you can overcook the inside. At too low a temperature, the inside could finish before the outside has the perfect sear.

A few words of advice: First, have your grid well oiled and clean before searing. When the grid is hot, you can rub it down with tongs and a paper towel splashed with vegetable oil. Second, cast iron needs to be oiled—or well seasoned—because, once you put your meat on, you don't move it until it is time to turn. I mention this because I prefer to use a cast iron grid for searing. Each bar of the grid will become superheated and will therefore sear, leaving tasty grill marks. The meat should release from the grid when the grill marks have cooked. Third, use only tongs or spatulas to move the meat. Never use a carving fork because it will release valuable juices needlessly! Speaking of juices, searing does not sear in the juices. The juices are retained only by your control of the temperature and your timing of the cook. Fourth, don't press burgers down on the grate. You will only push the juices out and make them too dry. Last, always let your grilled meat rest on a grid under tented foil for 10 to 15 minutes. This gives time for the juices to redistribute and is a must for juicy meat! If you follow these steps, you will have juicy and tender bites every time.

Some recipes call for searing, then roasting indirectly to finish. If you are cooking directly and your fire gets too hot, or if the meat is searing too quickly before the inside is cooked, you can always remove the meat from the Egg, close the vents and let it cool down. If the outside temperature is 70°F (21°C) or lower, a dome temperature of 750°F (399°C) can cool down to about 400°F (204°C) in about 20 minutes if both the top and bottom vents are closed. If it is hotter outside, it is more difficult to cool down the Egg. In that situation, it is best to sneak up on your searing temperature slowly and not overshoot it. The key is not to let the fire get too hot and intense. Consider searing at a dome temperature of 450°F (232°C) if you need to get the Egg to a lower temperature thereafter. You can also plan to sear after you have cooked other foods at a lower temperature. A patio umbrella will keep the Egg in the shade (and you, too!). You can also fill the firebox up one-quarter to one-third of the way before lighting; less charcoal will die down more quickly than a full firebox. As a last resort, you can place the hot coals in a small, covered metal garbage can placed on a noncombustible surface. I use one for all my ash when cleaning out my Eggs. With limited lit charcoal, you can leave the dome open to cool off the Egg. Do not put water in the Egg. Water can crack it or get into the porcelain and freeze and cause problems with the fire. All of this may sound complicated or cumbersome, but it really isn't. It is like driving a car. You don't always consciously put on your brake or step on the gas, but you stop and go just fine when necessary.

One huge word of caution is always to be prepared for flashback, especially when opening an Egg that was very hot when the dome was closed. Remember to burp it (see Chapter 1 on safety).

MARINATED BLADE STEAK

Blade steak is also known as "top blade steak" or "flat iron steak." The cut is from the chuck and has a line of gristle running down the middle. By cutting out the gristle, you end up with a really tender and relatively inexpensive piece of meat to grill. This recipe cooks the meat as a steak, but it is also very good for kabobs and stir-fries. It is very tender and accepts marinade well.

MAKES ABOUT 8 SERVINGS

3 pounds (1361g) blade steak

1 cup (237ml) olive oil

1 cup (237ml) soy sauce

½ cup (118ml) honey

1 tablespoon (15g) minced ginger

2 tablespoons (19g) minced garlic

½ cup (115g) brown sugar

¼ cup (60ml) apple cider vinegar

½ teaspoon fresh ground black pepper

Trim the gristle from the center of the steaks by cutting them in two. In a large bowl, mix the other ingredients together, and add the steaks. Refrigerate for 2 to 6 hours, turning occasionally.

Set up the Egg for 350°F (177°C) direct. With the top and bottom vents wide open, light the fire and close the Egg. When the dome temperature gets up to about 250°F (121°C), about 10 minutes, close the bottom screen. When the dome temperature approaches 350°F (177°C), about 5 minutes, slide the top of the daisy wheel partially closed, leaving it ¼ of the way open.

When the Egg is up to temperature, grill the steaks for 4 minutes, then flip and grill for another 3 minutes, to an internal temperature of 130°F (54°C). Remove from the Egg and place in a tent of aluminum foil on a rack to rest for 10 minutes before serving.

SPICED RIB EYE STEAK

The rib eye steak is essentially a boneless piece of prime rib. It is known for its tender, juicy and beefy qualities. These steaks are great cooked with just salt and pepper, but the rub adds additional flavors that work well with this thick cut, juicy steak. I adapted this method of searing from "T Rex" of the Big Green Egg online forum.

MAKES ABOUT 4 SERVINGS

4 rib eye steaks, 1½ inch (4 cm) thick, choice or higher grade

2 tablespoons (30ml) olive oil

¼ cup (30g) chili powder

1 tablespoon (15g) salt

2 teaspoons (4g) black pepper, coarsely ground

1 teaspoon (3g) garlic powder

1 teaspoon (3g) onion powder

½ tablespoon (5g) smoked paprika

4 tablespoons (57g) unsalted butter

Set the Egg for 700°F (371°C) direct. With the top and bottom vents wide open, light the fire and close the Egg. When the dome temperature gets up to about 250°F (121°C), about 10 minutes, close the bottom screen. When the dome temperature approaches 700°F (371°C), about 15 minutes, slide the top of the daisy wheel partially closed, keeping it ¾ of the way open. It will probably take between 20 and 30 minutes to get to 700°F (371°C).

Cut any outside fat from the edges of the steaks and rub them with olive oil. Mix together all the other ingredients though the paprika and apply to the steaks.

When the Egg is up to 700°F (371°C), place the steaks on the oiled cast iron grate. Sear for 1½ minutes, then rotate the steaks a quarter-turn for another minute. Flip the steaks and sear like you did the first side. Remove them from the Egg and let rest for 20 minutes.

Meanwhile, set the Egg for 400°F (204°C) indirect by adding the plate setter and shutting the vents to lower the temperature. When 20 minutes have passed, place the steaks back on, indirect. Close the dome and roast 4 minutes per side for medium rare. After the last flip, place a slice of unsalted butter on the top of each steak to melt. Remove from the Egg, tent with aluminum foil and let rest for 10 minutes before serving.

Note: Always burp the Egg when opening, especially when cooking over 400°F (204°C), to prevent flashback. See Chapter 1 on safety.

AWARD-WINNING COFFEE-ENCRUSTED PORK TENDERLOIN

Coffee actually makes a very good rub base for this recipe. The combination of the rub and marinade adds sweetness, a little tartness from the orange zest, enhanced orange flavors from the liqueurs and a background earthiness from the coffee. My cousin Tim DiFrancesco came up with the glaze for a competition, and I am glad he did!

MAKES ABOUT 6 SERVINGS

2 pork tenderloins

2 teaspoons (10ml) olive oil

ORANGE MARMALADE GLAZE

1 cup (240ml) orange marmalade

2 teaspoons (10ml) Grand Marnier

1 teaspoon (5ml) triple sec or Cointreau

1 teaspoon (5ml) soy sauce

COFFEE RUB

3 tablespoons (17g) ground coffee

1 tablespoon (20g) kosher or sea salt

1 tablespoon (12g) dark brown sugar

1 teaspoon (2g) ground black pepper

1 teaspoon (2g) garlic powder

1 teaspoon (3g) onion powder

(Instead of this rub, we also recommend ⅜ cup [90g] Dizzy Pig Red Eye Express®)

Mix all the marmalade glaze ingredients together and simmer over low heat until reduced by half, about 10 to 15 minutes. Mix all dry rub ingredients together.

Remove the silver skin from the tenderloins and rub them with olive oil. Rub the coffee rub on tenderloins and press into the meat. Cover with plastic wrap and let sit in the refrigerator for several hours or overnight.

Set the Egg for high heat, 500°F (260°C) direct. With the top and bottom vents wide open, light the fire and close the Egg. When the dome temperature gets up to about 250°F (121°C), about 10 minutes, close the bottom screen. When the dome temperature approaches 500°F (260°C), about 10 minutes, slide the top of the daisy wheel partially closed, keeping it halfway open.

Sear the tenderloins for one to two minutes per side. Remove the tenderloins and reduce the temperature of the Egg to 350°F to 375°F (177°C to 191°C). Return the meat to the Egg, dome closed, for about 10 minutes, turning twice. When the internal temperature reaches about 120°F (49°C), brush on the orange marmalade glaze. Continue cooking until the internal temperature reaches 135°F (57°C). Pork tenderloin is very lean and should not be cooked beyond 135°F (57°C) internal, or it will dry out and be tough. Remove, re-sauce, cover with foil and let rest for 15 to 20 minutes. The internal temperature should rise to 145°F (63°C). Cut into ½-inch (1.5-cm) slices and serve hot or cold.

(continued)

Note: Always burp the Egg when opening, especially when cooking over 400°F (204°C), to prevent flashback. See Chapter 1 on safety.

BOURBON SOY FLANK STEAK

Flank steak has a very pronounced flavor but is very tough. When cooked to medium rare, and sliced thinly—diagonally across the grain—it is very tender. If you don't overcook and you slice it thinly, it won't be tough. Flank steak is often used in fajitas and tacos, but it can be served on a salad or plated with potato salad or jicama slaw. This bourbon marinade is sweet, spicy and savory, and it makes the tender, beefy flank steak explode with flavor.

MAKES ABOUT 6 SERVINGS

2 pounds (900g) flank steak

2 tablespoons (19g) minced garlic

1 tablespoon (15ml) honey

½ cup (120ml) soy sauce

¼ cup (60ml) bourbon

1 teaspoon (2g) cayenne pepper

⅛ teaspoon black pepper, plus more to taste

Salt, to taste

Prepare the marinade by combining all ingredients except the steak in a small bowl, mixing well. Place the marinade in a 1-gallon (4L) resealable plastic freezer bag. Add the steak to the bag and massage the marinade into the meat. Marinate for 4 to 6 hours in the refrigerator, turning and massaging every hour.

Set up the Egg for 450°F (232°C) direct. With the top and bottom vents wide open, light the fire and close the Egg. When the dome temperature gets up to about 250°F (121°C), about 10 minutes, close the bottom screen. When the dome temperature approaches 450°F (232°C), about 10 minutes, slide the top of the daisy wheel partially closed, leaving it halfway open.

Take the steak from the marinade and discard the marinade. Season with salt and pepper. When the Egg is up to temperature, sear the steak for 5 minutes per side, until the internal temperature reaches 130°F (54°C). Because you are cooking direct, you can see how evenly the hot coals are lit in the firebox. Flank steak has a large surface area, so place it where the coals are burning the best for even cooking. If only part is over the hottest coals, rotate the steak halfway through the cook so that the whole underside gets seared. Remove from the Egg and tent with aluminum foil on a rack, resting the meat for 15 minutes. Slice thinly, diagonally across the grain, and serve.

Note: Always burp the Egg when opening, especially when cooking over 400°F (204°C), to prevent flashback. See Chapter 1 on safety.

CIDER-BRINED PORK CHOPS WITH PEACH SALSA

Most everyone I know grew up eating pork chops. They were usually pan fried, crisp on the outside and a little dry on the inside. For the past couple of decades, pork has become leaner and leaner. Chops now have very little fat, making them dry when cooked. Using brine helps them retain moisture, making them more tender and juicy. Do not leave them in the brine too long, or they will end up tougher and salty. You can infuse other flavors besides salt into the chop while you brine. Consider adding other spices to give different flavors.

MAKES ABOUT 4 SERVINGS

4 bone-in loin rib chops, 1½ inches (4 cm) thick

2 tablespoons (30ml) olive oil

¼ cup (30g) Pork Rub (page 208)

PEACH SALSA
1 cup (150g) diced peaches

¼ cup (38g) diced red onion

½ cup (25g) finely diced scallions

2 tablespoons (19g) minced garlic

1 cup (161g) diced tomatoes

½ teaspoon salt

½ teaspoon pepper, finely ground

2 tablespoons (30ml) lime juice

BRINE
2 cups (475ml) cold water, divided

¼ cup (60g) kosher salt

½ cup (100g) brown sugar

1 cup (237ml) cold apple cider or apple juice

Mix all the peach salsa ingredients together except the salt, pepper and lime; then add the salt, pepper and lime. Taste and adjust as desired. If it is too salty for your liking, add more tomatoes and peaches.

A few hours before cooking, make the brine by boiling one cup (236ml) water, then add the salt and sugar, stirring to dissolve. Remove from heat and let cool to room temperature. Add the remaining cold water and cold apple cider. Refrigerate the brine for at least one hour. Rinse off the chops and pat dry, removing any bone saw dust. Two hours before cook time, place the chops and the cold brine in a resealable 2-gallon (7.8-L) freezer bag. Refrigerate for 2 hours, turning every ½ hour.

Set up the Egg for 450°F (232°C) direct. With the top and bottom vents wide open, light the fire and close the Egg. When the dome temperature gets up to about 250°F (121°C), about 10 minutes, close the bottom screen. When the dome temperature approaches 450°F (232°C), about 10 minutes, slide the top of the daisy wheel partially closed, keeping it halfway open.

After 2 hours in the brine, remove the chops and rinse, then pat them dry. Coat with olive oil, then rub with pork rub.

When the Egg is up to temperature, sear the chops for 3 minutes per side, until caramelized. Remember to burp the Egg. Remove the chops and set up the Egg for 350°F (177°C) indirect with a drip pan. When the dome temperature approaches 350°F (177°C), slide the top of the daisy wheel partially closed, keeping the petals ¼ open.

When the Egg is back down to 350°F (177°C), place the chops back on and grill for 6 minutes total, flipping once, until the internal temperature reaches 135°F (57°C). Remove from the Egg and tent in aluminum foil on a rack to rest for 10 minutes. The rested internal temperature should read between 145°F and 150°F (63°C and 66°C).

Note: Always burp the Egg when opening, especially when cooking over 400°F (204°C), to prevent flashback. See Chapter 1 on safety.

CHAMPIONSHIP COFFEE-ENCRUSTED LAMB CHOPS

I never ate lamb chops as a kid. Well, maybe just once at Aunt Mary's house. We practiced these chops for a competition, and Mary Carmen, our Lebanese friend who grew up eating lamb, said they were the best she had ever tasted. Lamb has a pronounced flavor and is therefore suited for bold seasonings. This coffee rub pairs well with the tender lamb chops. The flavors and texture of these first-place chops will pleasantly surprise you!

MAKES ABOUT 6 SERVINGS

12 lamb chops, 1 inch (2.5cm) thick

2 tablespoons (30ml) olive oil

COFFEE RUB

3 tablespoons (17g) fresh ground coffee

1 tablespoon (20g) kosher or sea salt

1 tablespoon (12g) dark brown sugar

1 teaspoon (2g) ground black pepper

1 teaspoon (3g) garlic powder

1 teaspoon (3g) onion powder

(Instead of this rub, we also like ⅜ cup [90g] Dizzy Pig Red Eye Express®)

Mix all coffee rub ingredients together. Pat the chops dry and remove any bone saw dust, then add olive oil to the chops. Rub the coffee rub on all sides and press into the meat. Cover with plastic wrap and let sit in the refrigerator for several hours or overnight.

Set the Egg for high heat, 450°F (232°C) direct. With the top and bottom vents wide open, light the fire and close the Egg. When the dome temperature gets up to about 250°F (121°C), about 10 minutes, close the bottom screen. When the dome temperature approaches 450°F (232°C), about 10 minutes, slide the top of the daisy wheel partially closed, leaving it halfway open.

Sear the chops for 2 to 3 minutes per side. When the internal temperature reaches 125°F (52°C), remove from the Egg, cover with foil and let rest for 10 minutes before serving.

Note: Always burp the Egg when opening, especially when cooking over 400°F (204°C), to prevent flashback. See Chapter 1 on safety.

BASIC BEEF BURGERS

Beef burgers are like holidays: everyone has their favorite. There are so many ways to make burgers that we sometimes get away from a really good, basic burger. Fresh ground beef is important, but it doesn't need to be expensive. Ground chuck, with an 80-to-20 meat-to-fat ratio, has great flavor. Grind your own if you like. You can always save brisket fat trimmings and freeze them for use in your burger meat.

MAKES ABOUT 4 SERVINGS

1 pound (454g) freshly ground 80/20 chuck

2 teaspoons (10g) sea salt

1 teaspoon (2g) black pepper

4 slices gouda cheese

4 hamburger buns, toasted

Set up the Egg for 400°F (204°C) direct. With the top and bottom vents wide open, light the fire and close the Egg. When the dome temperature gets up to about 250°F (121°C), about 10 minutes, close the bottom screen. When the dome temperature approaches 400°F (204°C), about 10 minutes, slide the top of the daisy wheel partially closed, leaving it ¼ open.

Mix the salt and pepper into the ground meat, but do not over handle (it will make the burgers less juicy), making 4 patties. Place the burgers on the Egg and cook for 4 minutes on the first side, flip and cook for 3 minutes on the second side. Add a slice of cheese to each burger for the last 3 minutes. Remove from the heat and let rest for 5 minutes before serving.

Note: Always burp the Egg when opening, especially when cooking over 400°F (204°C), to prevent flashback. See Chapter 1 on safety. I keep the dome closed during cooking so the fire doesn't get hotter, to allow the top surface of the meat to cook at the same time as the bottom. With a direct cook, the grid temperature is hotter than the dome temperature; I only use the dome temperature as a reference. I know that if the coals are hot and well lit, and the dome temperature is at 400°F (204°C), the burgers will sear and cook as intended. You may need to move them around if coals are lit under the grid in more places than others.

SPICY APPLE PORK BURGERS

Pork burgers are a great change from beef burgers and can be just as juicy. The bacon and spices make these pork burgers unlike any beef burger. The crunch of the apple and the hint of mustard give great complementary taste and texture. For a surprising twist, add ¼-inch (6-mm) cubes of raw shrimp to the ground meat before mixing in the garlic spice mix.

MAKES ABOUT 4 SERVINGS

1 pound (454g) ground pork

¼ pound (113g) ground, thick-sliced, hickory-smoked bacon

1 tablespoon (9g) minced garlic

1 teaspoon (2g) allspice

½ teaspoon salt

½ teaspoon fresh ground black pepper

6 scallions, white and green parts, diced

1 tablespoon (15ml) olive oil

4 peeled apple slices

4 toasted hamburger buns

Yellow mustard to taste

Set up the Egg for 350°F (177°C) direct with a cast iron pan that fits into the Egg, including the handle. With the top and bottom vents wide open, light the fire and close the Egg. When the dome temperature gets up to about 250°F (121°C), about 10 minutes, close the bottom screen. When the dome temperature approaches 350°F (177°C), about 5 minutes, slide the top of the daisy wheel partially closed, leaving it ¼ of the way open.

In a small bowl, mix together the garlic, allspice, salt, pepper and scallions. In a larger bowl, place the ground pork and the ground bacon, then add the garlic spice mix. The meat should be cold when you start to mix it. If the fat in the bacon and pork gets too warm while mixing, the mixture will become mushy and the burgers dense. Be careful not to over-work the ground meat or it will become tough and less juicy. Mix only until the red bacon pieces are well dispersed. Use only your fingertips, and don't squeeze the meat in the palm of your hand. Form the burger mix into 4 patties, but do not over-pack!

Add the olive oil to the griddle pan and swirl to cover. Place the burgers in the pan and cook for 3 minutes per side, until the internal temperature of the meat reaches at least 165°F (74°C). Remove the patties from the Egg and let rest on a rack for 5 minutes.

While the burgers are resting, add the apple slices to the griddle pan and sear for 1½ minutes per side, until lightly wilted. Place the sliced hamburger buns on the griddle and toast for 1 minute. Place the burgers on the buns and top with an apple slice and a squirt of yellow mustard before adding the tops.

SULLY'S MARINATED STEAK TIPS

This recipe was contributed by Mike "Sully" Sullivan of Worcester, Massachusetts. Sully and his wife Terry have had their XL Egg since NewEgglandfest 2010. They make up part of the award-winning competition barbecue team Lunchmeat. Sully is well known in New England, as he has been an active member of the New England Barbecue Society (NEBS) for a number of years and has served on their Board of Directors for three terms. He is a NEBS contest Official, a Certified Barbecue Judge for the Kansas City Barbecue Society and has volunteered countless hours to charitable events in and around New England. You know Sully has arrived at a barbecue contest by his familiar yell of "Baaaaahbecuuuuuue!" heard throughout the grounds.

Steak tips are a Boston-area obsession. Many restaurants claim to have the best. The tips are marinated, and most supermarket meat counters have a large variety of flavors. When grilled directly, the sugars in the marinade caramelize and add a great taste. The inside is flavored by the marinade and provides a beefy bite. Sully got this "Best of Boston" recipe and has modified it for additional flavor. Sully uses Coca Cola®, but your favorite caramel-colored soft drink could be used. I would use Moxie®; you could use root beer or Pepsi®. Try your favorite and you can't go wrong.

MAKES ABOUT 12 SERVINGS

3 to 5 pounds (1.3 to 2.3 kg) of your favorite steak tips. Sully's favorite is hanging tender, but this recipe will work just as well with sirloin tips or flap meat.

2 cups (475ml) zesty Italian salad dressing; regular, NOT light

2 cups (475ml) Coca-Cola® (Don't use diet!)

1 (7-oz [198-g]) can chipotle in adobo sauce, finely chopped

¼ cup (38g) chopped garlic

1 (1.4 ounce [38-g]) package Latin seasoning (such as Sazón)

Black pepper to taste

Mix all marinade ingredients in a bowl. Trim any visible fat or silver skin from the steak tips and place the tips in a resealable freezer bag. Pour the marinade over the steak and seal the bag. Rub the marinade around to ensure all the tips get covered. Place in refrigerator for at least 8 hours, but 24 hours is best. Turn and flip the bag over every so often to ensure all the meat stays covered in the marinade.

Set the Egg for 400°F (204°C) direct. With the top and bottom vents wide open, light the fire and close the Egg. When the dome temperature gets up to about 250°F (121°C), about 10 minutes, close the bottom screen. When the dome temperature approaches 400°F (204°C), about 10 minutes, slide the top of the daisy wheel partially closed, leaving it ¼ of the way open.

Grill steaks to about 160°F (71°C) internal. Let rest for 10 minutes before serving. Your friends & family will be begging for more!

Note: Always burp the Egg when opening, especially when cooking over 400°F (204°C), to prevent flashback. See Chapter 1 on safety.

GRILLED CHICKEN OR BEEF TERIYAKI

Chicken and beef teriyaki are my favorite appetizers whenever we eat out. The quality and flavor, however, are usually hit-or-miss. Making your own will ensure that you always get the right balance between sweet and savory and crisp and moist. Homemade teriyaki sauce is far better than store-bought. This recipe tastes fresher and brighter than from a bottle. As an alternative, try using bone-in chicken thighs or beef flap meat (sirloin tip).

MAKES ABOUT 6 SERVINGS

2 pounds (900g) boneless chicken thighs or flank steak

1 cup (240ml) soy sauce

½ cup (120ml) mirin

¼ cup (50g) brown sugar

2 tablespoons (19g) chopped garlic

1 tablespoon (19g) chopped or grated ginger

1 tablespoon (15ml) sesame oil

12 (8-inch [20-cm]) metal or wooden skewers

Combine all ingredients except the meat, mixing well, and place in doubled-up 1-gallon (0.9-L) freezer bags. If using chicken, remove any visible fat or silver skin. Do not slice. If using flank steak, cut it into 1½-inch (4-cm) strips across the grain and remove any visible fat or silver skin. (For food safety, don't ever put raw chicken in the same container as any other meat.) Once trimmed, place the meat in the plastic bag, remove as much air as possible, and seal. Marinate in the refrigerator for at least four hours, or overnight, turning and massaging a few times.

Set up the Egg for 350°F (177°C) direct. With the top and bottom vents wide open, light the fire and close the Egg. When the dome temperature gets up to about 250°F (121°C), about 10 minutes, close the bottom screen. When the dome temperature approaches 350°F (177°C), about 5-10 minutes, slide the top of the daisy wheel partially closed, leaving it ¼ of the way open.

Take the meat out of the bag and discard the marinade. Thread the chicken or beef on a skewer. If the chicken doesn't stick well on one skewer, use two. Place the skewers on an oiled grid, close the dome and cook to an internal temperature of at least 165°F (74°C), about ½ an hour. Turn the meat often to make sure the sugar in the marinade doesn't burn. A little char is okay!

Serve on the skewers. As an alternative, you can cook to the above temperature and slice into 1½-inch (4-cm) pieces and serve without skewers.

This recipe cooks direct because the meat is thin and I want a little caramelizing of the sugars on the surface. If the meat were thicker, I would cook indirect to prevent the sugars from burning.

ROASTED BEEF TENDERLOIN

Beef tenderloin is renowned for its tender and buttery texture. The flavor, however, is a bit lacking. Salting the roast about an hour ahead of cooking helps add flavor, as does searing and roasting on a charcoal fire. The best place to buy whole tenderloins is at a wholesale club. If you don't want to pay for whole tenderloin, ask the butcher to give you a 4-pound (1.8 kg) roast from the butt end. It will be larger than the rest of the tenderloin and will cook more evenly.

MAKES ABOUT 12 SERVINGS

1 (4-pound [1814g]) beef tenderloin, butt end

1 tablespoon (15g) kosher salt

2 tablespoons (30ml) olive oil

1 tablespoon (3g) black pepper

4 tablespoons (57g) compound butter (recipe below)

COMPOUND BUTTER

2 tablespoons (29g) unsalted butter, softened

1 tablespoon (15g) minced shallots

1 tablespoon (2g) minced parsley

Pinch of salt

Pinch of pepper

Trim the tenderloin of all fat, sinew and silver skin using a boning knife. When finished, rub salt all over the roast and let it sit at room temperature for one hour, covered with plastic wrap.

Mix together all the ingredients in the compound butter and set aside.

Set up the Egg for 450°F (232°C) direct. With the top and bottom vents wide open, light the fire and close the Egg. When the dome temperature gets up to about 250°F (121°C), about 10 minutes, close the bottom screen. When the dome temperature approaches 450°F (232°C), about 10 minutes, slide the top of the daisy wheel partially closed, leaving it halfway open.

After the butt has salted for one hour, rub it with olive oil and then pepper. When the Egg is up to temperature, sear the tenderloin on each side for 2 minutes, turning a quarter turn each time. After 8 minutes of searing, remove the tenderloin from the Egg and set up the Egg for 350°F (177°C) indirect with a drip pan. When the temperature is down to 350°F (177°C), place the roast back on the Egg, dome closed, for 20 minutes, until the internal temperature reaches 125°F (52°C). Remove the roast from the Egg and spoon the compound butter on the top of the roast. Tent under aluminum foil on a rack, letting it rest for 45 minutes. To serve, cut into ½-inch (1.5-cm) thick medallions.

Note: Always burp the Egg when opening, especially when cooking over 400°F (204°C), to prevent flashback. See Chapter 1 on safety.

CHAPTER 5

ONE IN THE OVEN

USING YOUR BIG GREEN EGG AS AN AMAZING CERAMIC OVEN

The Big Green Egg makes a great ceramic oven because it retains heat and moisture very well. Baking is done indirectly, as with roasting in Chapter 3. Temperature and time will be similar to those of your kitchen oven, and you can use similar racks, baking sheets, casserole dishes and cast iron cookware.

There are a few notable differences between baking in your oven and baking in the Big Green Egg. First, you can bake all day in the Egg and never overheat your kitchen. Second, more moisture is retained when baking on the Egg than in your oven. Third, a little hint of smoky flavor from the lump charcoal adds an earthy note to your baked goods that you just can't get with an oven. Last, you can have a pizza party with the Egg and not bake pizza after pizza at 600°F (316°C) in your kitchen!

Just as with roasting, baking is best "up in the dome" for uniform cooking. You can bake indirectly at the grid level, but it is better to cook on a raised grid above the grid level to allow for more even heat circulation under and around your food. Remember to rotate the food at least once during your cook to compensate for hot spots. Baking in multiple layers within the Egg works well, provided you move and rotate your food during cooking.

ITALIAN COLD CUT STROMBOLI

This recipe is very versatile. You may substitute meats and cheeses to your own taste with the same great results. The dough will bake well in the Egg and is certainly something different to try. We often make them for our demonstrations. You can double or triple the recipe and cook a few at a time.

MAKES 4 TO 6 SERVINGS

1 pound (454g) store-made pizza dough

8 to 10 slices smoked ham

8 to 10 slices smoked turkey

8 to 10 slices genoa salami

1 jar roasted red peppers (water packed)

8 to 10 slices provolone cheese

Olive oil

Italian seasoning or your favorite rub

Cooking spray

Prepare the grill for 400°F (204°C) indirect. With the top and bottom vents wide open, light the fire and close the Egg. When the dome temperature gets up to about 250°F (121°C), about 10 minutes, close the bottom screen. When the dome temperature approaches 400°F (204°C), about 5-10 minutes, slide the top of the daisy wheel partially closed, leaving it ¼ of the way open.

Roll out pizza dough on a lightly floured surface to form a thin, rectangular crust, about 11 by 13 inches (28 by 33 cm). Layer slices of meat, peppers and cheese down the center of the crust, ending with cheese.

Using a knife or kitchen shears, cut both sides of the crust next to the meat and cheese filling, making several 1-inch (2.5-cm) strips. Fold in each end of the crust over the filling. Criss-cross the cut strips to cover the filling. Brush olive oil on top and sprinkle with Italian seasoning or your favorite rub.

Spray a piece of foil with cooking spray and place stromboli on it. Close the dome and bake for 15 to 20 minutes, or until crust turns golden brown. As an alternative, you can cook it on a pre-heated pizza stone.

Remove to a wire rack and let rest for about 10 minutes before slicing.

MAPLE SKILLET CORNBREAD

Cornbread is great for breakfast, lunch or dinner. This recipe combines sweet with heat. Dumping the batter into a hot skillet makes a tasty crust form at the bottom. For variety, try adding dried cranberries or whole corn kernels. If you're really in the mood, fry some bacon to add to the batter and use the bacon fat instead of butter.

MAKES 6 TO 8 SERVINGS

1 cup (170g) yellow cornmeal

1 cup (125g) all-purpose flour

½ teaspoon baking soda

1 teaspoon (4g) baking powder

1 teaspoon (4g) sugar

½ teaspoon salt

2 eggs, lightly beaten

1 cup (240ml) milk

⅓ cup (80ml) maple syrup

4 tablespoons (60ml) unsalted butter, melted—divided

2 jalapeño peppers, minced, seeds and ribs removed

Set the Egg for 400°F (204°C) direct. With the top and bottom vents wide open, light the fire and close the Egg. When the dome temperature gets up to about 250°F (121°C), about 10 minutes, close the bottom screen. When the dome temperature approaches 400°F (204°C), about 10 minutes, slide the top of the daisy wheel partially closed, leaving it ¼ of the way open.

Preheat a 10-inch (25-cm) cast iron skillet. While the skillet is heating, whisk together the cornmeal, flour, baking soda, baking powder, sugar and salt in a large bowl. In a separate bowl, mix together the beaten eggs, milk, maple syrup, half of the melted butter and the minced jalapeño. Add the wet ingredients to the dry and mix together.

Using heat-protective gloves, carefully remove the heated skillet from the Egg. Add the other half of the butter to coat the skillet, then pour in the batter. Place the skillet back in the Egg and cook for about 20 minutes, until a toothpick comes out clean.

KIM'S MEXICAN CHICKEN CASSEROLE

This recipe was contributed by Kim and Ginny Youngblood of Lawrenceville, Georgia. They have been "Eggers" for more than seven years. They teach Big Green Egg cooking classes, do demonstration cooks at stores in the Southeast, and cook at five or six Eggfests throughout the country each year. Kim has won several awards for his recipes. We speak for all Eggheads in the Northeast when we say we really look forward to Kim and Ginny's creations at NewEgglandfest every summer! This is a great chicken casserole recipe, utilizing ingredients easily available, and it is quick to put together while your Egg comes up to temperature. It is creamy and gooey with cheese, and it has just the right amount of heat when prepared as written.

MAKES 8 TO 10 SERVINGS

4 cups (1L) cooked, chopped chicken (3 to 4 breast halves)

2 cups (421g) instant rice

1 (10.75-oz [318-ml]) can cream of chicken soup

1 cup (240ml) sour cream

½ cup (76g) diced onion

1 10-oz (296ml) can tomatoes with chilis, such as Ro*Tel®

1 tablespoon (10g) diced green chilis (more or less, to taste)

1 tablespoon (15ml) chipotle peppers in adobo sauce, chopped fine (more or less, to taste)

¼ teaspoon cumin

½ teaspoon garlic powder

Salt and pepper to taste

1½ cups (375ml) chicken broth

12 ounces (340g) shredded cheddar cheese, divided

Chopped cilantro

Set the Egg to 350°F (177°C) indirect. With the top and bottom vents wide open, light the fire and close the Egg. When the dome temperature gets up to about 250°F (121°C), about 10 minutes, close the bottom screen. When the dome temperature approaches 350°F (177°C), about 5-10 minutes, slide the top of the daisy wheel partially closed, leaving it ¼ of the way open.

Cut the cooked chicken into bite-size pieces and combine in a large bowl with all ingredients and half of the cheese. Mix well. Pour into a greased 9 by 13-inch (23 by 33-cm) casserole dish and sprinkle the remainder of the cheese on top. Cook until the cheese on top starts to bubble, 25 to 30 minutes. Sprinkle with cilantro before serving.

SMOKIN' ACES PIZZA

This recipe was contributed by Chuck and Nancy Helwig of the Smokin' Aces Competition Team from Chicopee, Massachusetts. In 2006, they decided to buy a Big Green Egg, and so began their obsession with the cooker. Currently, they are the proud owners of six Eggs of various sizes. Shortly after acquiring their first Egg, Chuck and Nancy wanted to try competition barbecue, so Smokin' Aces was born. They took a competition class offered by the New England Barbecue Society, and Cindi and I were their instructors. Since that day, we have been lucky to have Chuck and Nancy as our friends. This year, 2014, Smokin' Aces the Rhode Island State Champions and headed down to the Jack Daniel's Invitational Barbecue Championships in Lynchburg, Tennessee. Chuck and Nancy have made countless pizzas in the Big Green Egg in grilling competitions, at cooking demos, and on their deck at home. Nothing beats the taste of a wood-fired pizza. This is one of the pizzas they frequently make, but you can substitute any toppings you like.

MAKES 6 TO 8 SERVINGS

PIZZA DOUGH (MAKES TWO CRUSTS)
4¼ cups (531g) flour

2¼ teaspoons (7g) instant yeast, or one pack of yeast

1½ teaspoons (9g) salt

2 teaspoons (8g) sugar

2 tablespoons (30ml) olive oil

1¾ cups (414ml) warm water

TOPPINGS
Pesto sauce (a store-bought brand saves time)

Mozzarella cheese

Grilled asparagus

Roma tomato

Red pepper relish (a store-bought brand saves time)

Put all dry ingredients into a food processor with the dough hook on. Pulse the dry ingredients 3 or 4 times. Turn on the food processor and slowly add the olive oil, then slowly add the warm water until a ball forms and the dough is sticky to the touch. Turn off the food processor and let the dough rest for 2 minutes. Turn on the food processor again for 30 to 40 seconds, then place the dough in a well-oiled bowl and let rise. If you plan to use the dough the next day, place it in an oiled resealable bag and put it in the refrigerator, where it will rise overnight.

With the top and bottom vents wide open, light the fire and close the Egg. When the dome temperature gets up to about 250°F (121°C), about 10 minutes, close the bottom screen. When the dome temperature approaches 550°F (288°C), about 10-15 minutes, slide the top of the daisy wheel partially closed, keeping it halfway open.

To grill the asparagus, lightly coat it in olive oil and place on the grill for a few minutes.

For the Egg setup you will not need your grill grate. Put the plate setter in the Egg with the legs down and place a pizza stone on top. To prevent the pizza from sticking, let the plate setter and stone warm to temperature before putting the pizza on to cook, between 550°F (288°C) and 600°F (316°C).

Flour a cutting board and roll out your risen crust. Spread cornmeal on a pizza peel and carefully lift the crust onto it. Spread on the pesto sauce, cover with mozzarella, and then arrange your asparagus in a wagon-wheel formation. Place thin slices of fresh Roma tomato between the "spokes." Finally, sprinkle red pepper relish over the top. Open your Egg and carefully slide the pizza off of the peel onto the pizza stone using a slight shaking motion.

Close the cover and check after about 6 minutes. You may need to reposition the pizza for even cooking. When it is done, slide it back onto the peel and transfer to a cutting board. Allow it to cool for a few minutes before slicing.

PEACH BREAD PUDDING WITH RUM SAUCE

Bread pudding may have been developed as a humble way to use up stale bread while providing a comforting dessert. It can be embellished so that it is a hearty, sweet and spicy dish unto itself. The peaches and dried cranberries add great texture and complement the custard with sweet and tart flavors. Add the spicy, sweet sauce and all your senses will be delighted!

MAKES 6 TO 8 SERVINGS

RUM SAUCE

1 cup (230g) unsalted butter

1 cup (240ml) heavy cream

1 cup (192g) sugar

½ cup (120ml) spiced or dark rum

½ cup (60g) chopped pecans

1 tablespoon (15ml) vanilla extract

PUDDING

1 quart (1L) half-and-half

3 large eggs, beaten

½ cup (115g) brown sugar

3 tablespoons (45ml) maple syrup

1 tablespoon (7g) cinnamon

1 tablespoon (15ml) vanilla extract

4 cups (200g) stale French bread, ½-inch (1.5-cm) cubes

1 cup (225g) sliced, peeled peaches

1 cup (120g) dried cranberries

¼ cup (57g) butter, softened

To make the rum sauce, melt the butter in a medium saucepan over medium heat until it starts to turn light brown, about 5 minutes. Add the remaining ingredients and bring to a simmer, stirring to dissolve the sugar. Cook for about 10 more minutes, until the sauce thickens, stirring frequently. Remove from the heat.

Set up the Egg for a dome temperature of 350°F (177°C) indirect. With the top and bottom vents wide open, light the fire and close the Egg. When the dome temperature gets up to about 250°F (121°C), about 10 minutes, close the bottom screen. When the dome temperature approaches 350°F (177°C), about 5-10 minutes, slide the top of the daisy wheel partially closed, leaving it ¼ of the way open.

For the custard, stir together the half-and-half, eggs, brown sugar, maple syrup, cinnamon and vanilla in a large bowl. Add the cubed bread, peaches and cranberries and gently combine.

Butter a 9 by 13-inch (33 by 23-cm) baking dish and pour the mixture into it. When the Egg is up to 350°F (177°C), bake the pudding for about 45 minutes, until it is golden on top and firm in the center. Spoon the pudding into dishes and serve warm, drizzled with rum sauce.

Note: When baking at 350°F (177°C), there is no need to adjust the vents to maintain a dome temperature of 350°F (177°C) once the food has been placed in the Egg. It should recover quickly and maintain the 350°F (177°C) dome temperature.

BOURBON PECAN PIE

You can't get much more Southern than pecan pie, but you don't need to be in the South to enjoy it. When cooked properly, the filling should be creamy and the crust flaky, with crunchy pecans and the sweetness of the corn syrup and sugars balanced by a little salt. In this recipe, the bourbon and vanilla combine well with the earthy tone of the dark brown sugar. Kid you not, this is a sweet dessert, but the rich, deep flavors and textures of the crust, pecans and filling make for a rewarding bite!

MAKES 6 TO 8 SERVINGS

3 eggs, lightly beaten

¾ cup (180ml) dark corn syrup

½ cup (100g) dark brown sugar

½ cup (96g) granulated sugar

4 tablespoons (57g) unsalted butter, softened

2 tablespoons (30ml) bourbon

1 teaspoon (5ml) vanilla extract

½ teaspoon salt

1 cup (120g) chopped pecans

1 (9-inch [22-cm]) piecrust

Butter for the pie plate

Set the Egg for 375°F (191°C) indirect with a raised grate. With the top and bottom vents wide open, light the fire and close the Egg. When the dome temperature gets up to about 250°F (121°C), about 10 minutes, close the bottom screen. When the dome temperature approaches 375°F (191°C), about 5-10 minutes, slide the top of the daisy wheel partially closed, leaving it ¼ of the way open.

In a large bowl, lightly beat the eggs and blend in the corn syrup. Add the sugars, butter, bourbon, vanilla extract and salt and blend together. Fold in the chopped pecans. Place the piecrust in a buttered pie plate and trim the edges. Pour in the pecan mix and spread evenly on the crust.

When the Egg is up to temperature, place the pie on a raised rack, close the dome and cook for about 40 minutes, until the outside is set and the center jiggles slightly. Remove from the Egg and let cool for 2 hours. Serve at room temperature.

MAPLE CRÈME BRÛLÉE

This crème brûlée recipe has done well for us in competition, winning a perfect 180 score at the largest barbecue competition in the world, The American Royal World Series of Barbecue in 2009. It's the perfect balance of creaminess, sweetness and crackly sugar crust, and it can easily be doubled for a crowd!

MAKES 9 SERVINGS

3 cups (710ml) heavy cream, divided

1 cup (130g) powdered sugar

½ cup (120ml) maple syrup

1 vanilla bean

9 egg yolks

9 teaspoons (57g) turbinado sugar

9 ramekins, 4-ounce (120ml) size

Propane or blow torch

Place half of the cream in a small saucepan with the sugar, maple syrup and vanilla bean. Slowly bring the temperature up until the milk is almost to the scalding point. Let the mixture rest for 10 to 15 minutes to extract the flavor from the vanilla bean. Whisk the egg yolks with the remaining cream and slowly stir into the heated mixture. Strain all of the above into a small pitcher, removing the vanilla bean.

Set the Egg for 300°F (149°C) indirect. With the top and bottom vents wide open, light the fire and close the Egg. When the dome temperature gets up to about 250°F (121°C), about 10 minutes, close the bottom screen. When the dome temperature approaches 300°F (149°C), about 5 minutes, slide the top of the daisy wheel closed, keeping the petals all the way open.

Place a raised rack on the grate. Line the bottom of a deep baking dish with a kitchen towel to help stabilize the ramekins, and add at least 2 inches (5 cm) of boiling water. Pour the custard mixture into the ramekins and carefully place them in the hot water bath. The ramekins should not touch one another, nor the sides of the pan. Bake until the internal temperature reaches between 170°F and 175°F (77°C and 79°C). Begin checking them after 40 minutes. Remove from heat and cool them on a rack, then cover tightly with plastic wrap and refrigerate until cold, at least 4 hours.

If condensation has occurred when you uncover the ramekins, carefully dab the custard with a paper towel to soak up the moisture. Sprinkle each with about 1 teaspoon (6g) of turbinado sugar, tilting and tapping the ramekin for even coverage. Ignite your torch to caramelize the sugar; and return ramekins, uncovered, to the refrigerator to re-chill, 30 to 45 minutes.

BLUEBERRY BUCKLE

My grandfather Wallace, my aunts, uncles, cousins, siblings and I used to make a family trip to a hillside blueberry patch in Unity, New Hampshire—owned by a Swedish fellow named Jon—to pick high-bush blueberries. These blueberries were smaller and sweeter than the cultivated blueberries available today. My parents would pick 30 to 40 quarts a day. My cousins Matt, Mark, Kenny, Kevin and I would pick a lot, but only about 2 quarts made it into the bin: they mostly ended in our bellies! All of my family made blueberry buckle. The following was my mother Madeline's recipe. It is very moist with a sweet crunch in the topping. It is great for breakfast, lunch or dinner!

MAKES 12 TO 16 SERVINGS

TOPPING

¼ cup (48g) granulated sugar

¼ cup (50g) light brown sugar

⅓ cup (41g) flour

½ teaspoon cinnamon

¼ cup (57g) unsalted butter, room temperature

BATTER

¾ cup (150g) granulated sugar

¼ cup (48g) vegetable shortening

1 large egg

½ cup (120ml) milk

2 cups (220g) flour

2 teaspoons (15g) baking powder

½ teaspoon salt

2 cups (200g) blueberries, fresh or frozen

In a medium bowl, combine the sugars, flour and cinnamon. With a pastry cutter or two forks, cut in the butter until the topping is crumbly.

Set the Egg for 375°F (191°C) indirect. With the top and bottom vents wide open, light the fire and close the Egg. When the dome temperature gets up to about 250°F (121°C), about 10 minutes, close the bottom screen. When the dome temperature approaches 375°F (191°C), about 5-10 minutes, slide the top of the daisy wheel partially closed, leaving it ¼ of the way open.

In a large bowl, thoroughly mix the sugar, shortening and egg. Stir in the milk. Sift together the flour, baking powder and salt. Add the sifted ingredients to the batter and mix just until combined. Gently stir in the blueberries. Spread the batter in a greased 9 by 13-inch (23 by 33-cm) baking dish. Sprinkle the topping over the batter. Bake on a raised rack in the Egg for 40 to 45 minutes with the dome closed, or until a toothpick inserted in the center comes out clean.

SPINACH AND FETA STUFFED BREAD

This recipe was contributed by Tim and Wendy Boucher of the Feeding Friendz Competition BBQ team from Deerfield, New Hampshire. They started competing in 2005. Over the past 10 years, they have won several Grand Championships and have been fortunate enough to be invited twice to The Jack Daniel's Invitational World Barbecue Championship in Lynchburg, Tennessee in 2010 and 2011. In 2013 they made it to the finals of the Sam's Club National Barbecue Tour, finishing with a second place brisket and thirteenth overall! Tim and Wendy love to feed their friends, Cindi and me included. Easy to put together, this stuffed bread recipe is a great go-to meal that can easily be doubled to feed a crowd. The ranch dressing adds lots of flavor to the baked bread, and the feta cheese is a creamy accompaniment to the chopped chorizo and spinach leaves.

SERVES 4–6

1 pound (454g) frozen bread dough, thawed

½ cup (120ml) ranch dressing

1 pound (454g) baby spinach leaves

8 ounces (225g) feta cheese, crumbled

1 stick chorizo, sliced and cut into small pieces

Nonstick cooking spray

Set the Egg to 350°F (177°C) indirect. With the top and bottom vents wide open, light the fire and close the Egg. When the dome temperature gets up to about 250°F (121°C), about 10 minutes, close the bottom screen. When the dome temperature approaches 350°F (177°C), about 5-10 minutes, slide the top of the daisy wheel partially closed, leaving it ¼ of the way open.

Roll the dough on a lightly floured surface into a 12-inch (30.5-cm) circle. Pour the ranch dressing on the dough and spread across with the back of a spoon. Cover the dressing with the baby spinach, the more the better: it will reduce as it bakes. Top with feta cheese and chorizo pieces.

Roll the dough into a log, turning in the side edges as you roll. Don't be afraid to stretch the dough to make everything fit. Wet the edges with water and pinch together to seal. Shape it by hand into a log shape.

Spray a foil pan with nonstick cooking spray and place the log in it. Cover and cook for about 30 minutes, then uncover and cook until the top is golden brown. Remove from the Egg and let cool for about 10 minutes before slicing. Serve and enjoy!

VARIATION: STEAK AND CHEESE STUFFED BREAD

MAKES 4 TO 6 SERVINGS

1 pound (450g) frozen bread dough, thawed

1½ pounds (680g) shaved steak

1 pound (227g) shredded cheese, divided (we like pepper jack)

Salt and pepper

Sauté the shaved steak prior to assembling. Using the same instructions as above, cover the dough with half of the cheese. Add the sautéed steak and top with the remainder of the cheese. Salt and pepper generously, roll to a log and cook as above.

MIXED FRUIT CROSTADA

Growing up, we always had fresh fruit: blackberries and cultivated raspberries from our own yard, or fruits at Uncle Sid's farm and at my cousin's Walhowdon Farm. These fruit tarts are called crostadas, galettes or croustades. By any name, they are delicious and easy to make. You can use any fruit you like. Taste your fruits for sweetness and tartness and adjust the sugar and lime juice accordingly. Serve them warm with a dollop of real whipped cream. The fruit provides the right mix of sweet and tart, with a flaky pie crust and a crunch from the almonds.

MAKES ABOUT 8 SERVINGS

PIECRUST (OR YOU MAY USE A PRE-MADE CRUST)

1½ cups (187g) all-purpose flour

1 teaspoon (4g) sugar

½ teaspoon salt

½ cup (115g) cold, unsalted butter cut into ¼-inch (6-mm) cubes

3 tablespoons (45ml) ice water

TOPPING

1 nectarine, cut into ½-inch (1.5-cm) pieces

½ cup (75g) blackberries

½ cup (75g) raspberries

½ cup (75g) blueberries

5 tablespoons (95g) turbinado sugar

1 tablespoon (15ml) lime juice

¼ cup (43g) sliced almonds

If you are using homemade piecrust, combine the flour, sugar and salt in a large bowl until well blended. Cut in the butter using two knives or a pastry blender, until the dough is the consistency of cornmeal, with the butter the size of small peas. Add the cold water and mix by hand just until the dough forms; don't overwork it. If it is too dry, add another tablespoon (15ml) of water. Alternatively, you may use a food processor. Either way, form the dough into a 5-inch (12.5cm) disk, wrap in plastic wrap and refrigerate for 30 to 60 minutes.

Set the Egg for 400°F (204°C) indirect with a raised grid and a pizza stone. With the top and bottom vents wide open, light the fire and close the Egg. When the dome temperature gets up to about 250°F (121°C), about 10 minutes, close the bottom screen. When the dome temperature approaches 400°F (204°C), about 10 minutes, slide the top of the daisy wheel partially closed, leaving it ¼ of the way open.

In a large bowl, mix together the fruit, sugar and lime juice. Place the chilled dough on a 14-inch (35-cm) piece of parchment paper and roll it out to a 12-inch (30-cm) circle, about ¼ inch (6 mm) thick. A perfect circle isn't necessary. Place the fruit mixture in the center of the dough, spreading it to within 3 inches (7.5 cm) of the edge. Lift and fold the 3-inch (7.5-cm) outer edge of the dough up and over the fruit mixture, cinching every so often, until all of the dough has been turned in. Sprinkle the sliced almonds on top.

When the Egg is up to temperature, place the crostada with the parchment paper onto the heated pizza stone. Close the dome and bake for 50 to 60 minutes, until the crust is golden brown, giving a quarter-turn every 15 minutes. When cooked, remove from the Egg with two large spatulas for support and place on a cooling rack for 5 minutes before slicing and serving.

SOUTHERN CORN PUDDING

Corn is my favorite vegetable, and I have always enjoyed a good creamed corn. Our first time to the Jack Daniel's Invitational World Barbecue Championship in Lynchburg, Tennessee, we ate at Miss Mary Bobo's for a family-style dinner. I had corn pudding for the first time, and I was in Heaven! Who cares about the contest? I met corn pudding! Every time I go to the Jack, I must have corn pudding. It is sweet and creamy custard with crisp corn kernels. It complements any meal! For a little kick, add a pinch of cayenne pepper or red pepper flakes.

MAKES ABOUT 12 SERVINGS

6 ears fresh corn, husked, with silk removed

2 cups (475ml) half-and-half

3 eggs, beaten

3 tablespoons (42g) unsalted butter, melted, plus more for the pan

1 tablespoon (19g) sugar

1 teaspoon (6g) salt

½ teaspoon (1g) nutmeg

Cut the corn kernels off the ears and place in a large bowl. Scrape the cobs with the back of the knife to get all remaining pulp.

Set the Egg for 350°F (177°C) indirect. With the top and bottom vents wide open, light the fire and close the Egg. When the dome temperature gets up to about 250°F (121°C), about 10 minutes, close the bottom screen. When the dome temperature approaches 350°F (177°C), about 5-10 minutes, slide the top of the daisy wheel partially closed, leaving it ¼ of the way open.

In a medium bowl, mix together the half-and-half and the beaten eggs. Stir in the melted butter. Add the sugar, salt and nutmeg and stir to combine. Add the liquid mixture to the corn and blend well. Pour the whole mixture into a well-buttered 9 by 9-inch (23 by 23-cm) baking dish.

When the Egg is up to temperature, place the pudding in the Egg, close the dome and bake for 35 to 40 minutes, until it has just set but isn't yet too firm. Remove to a rack and let rest for 5 minutes.

HERMITS

Hermits got their name because they can be stored for long periods. Fishermen in the North Atlantic brought them on their long excursions at sea. Hermits have molasses and spices like gingersnaps, but they are less sweet and are thicker and chewier than gingersnaps. The spicy mix is crispy on the outside, chewy on the inside. Though hermits taste better after they have been aged a few days, I admit that I don't have enough self control to wait.

MAKES ABOUT 24 BARS

½ cup (115g) unsalted butter, softened

½ cup (96g) sugar

½ cup (101g) dark brown sugar

½ cup (120ml) molasses

2 eggs, beaten

3 cups (375g) all-purpose flour

1 teaspoon (8g) baking powder

1 teaspoon (4g) baking soda

1 teaspoon (2g) salt

1 teaspoon (2g) allspice

1 teaspoon (2g) cinnamon

1 cup (152g) raisins

½ cup (58g) chopped walnuts

Cinnamon sugar for sprinkling (optional)

Set up the Egg for 350° (180°C) indirect. With the top and bottom vents wide open, light the fire and close the Egg. When the dome temperature gets up to about 250°F (121°C), about 10 minutes, close the bottom screen. When the dome temperature approaches 350°F (177°C), about 5-10 minutes, slide the top of the daisy wheel partially closed, leaving it ¼ of the way open.

In a large bowl, cream together the butter and sugars until smooth. Add the molasses and eggs and continue to mix well until combined. In a separate bowl, whisk together the flour, baking powder, baking soda, salt, allspice and cinnamon. Add to the wet ingredients and mix well. Fold in the raisins and walnuts.

On a large, greased baking pan, spread the batter in a smooth layer. Bake at 350°F (177°C) for 15 to 20 minutes, until the bars are done to your desired crispiness or chewiness. While still hot, sprinkle with a cinnamon-sugar mixture if you like. Let cool on a rack, then cut into 2 by 2-inch (5 by 5-cm) bars.

BLUEBERRY SCONES

Scones are less sweet and more dense than turnovers, but sweeter than biscuits. I think of them as more of a dessert than a biscuit. I like them hot or cold with coffee, tea or hot apple cider. Different fruits can be added if you wish.

MAKES 8 SERVINGS

2 cups (250g) all-purpose flour

1 tablespoon (23g) baking powder

¼ cup (48g) sugar

¼ teaspoon salt

6 tablespoons (86g) unsalted butter, chilled and cut into ¼-inch (6-mm) cubes

1 cup (240ml) heavy cream

1 cup (100g) fresh blueberries

Set the Egg for 375°F (191°C) indirect. With the top and bottom vents wide open, light the fire and close the Egg. When the dome temperature gets up to about 250°F (121°C), about 10 minutes, close the bottom screen. When the dome temperature approaches 375°F (191°C), about 5-10 minutes, slide the top of the daisy wheel partially closed, leaving it ¼ of the way open.

In a medium bowl, mix the flour, baking powder, sugar and salt until well blended. Add the chilled butter and fold in until well dispersed. Add the cream and fold in the blueberries. Do not over-mix the ingredients. They should be loosely combined, but not in a paste like a dough ball; they should maintain some of their individual texture. Place the dough on a floured surface and press flat into a circle about 1 inch (2.5cm) thick. Cut the circle into 8 wedges and separate the wedges. Sprinkle the tops with sugar. On a greased pan, bake the scones at 375°F (191°C) for about 20 minutes, until the tops are golden brown. Remove from the Egg and let cool on a rack for 10 minutes.

CRANBERRY OATMEAL COOKIES

Crunchy oatmeal cookies are probably my favorite cookie. I really enjoy the crispy outside and chewy inside. Raisins are customary in these cookies, but I really prefer the sweet tartness of dried cranberries, which are plentiful in New England.

MAKES 12 TO 16 COOKIES

1 cup (125g) all-purpose flour
2 cups (161g) rolled oats
1 cup (230g) light brown sugar
1 cup (192g) granulated sugar
⅛ teaspoon cinnamon
½ teaspoon salt
¼ teaspoon nutmeg
½ teaspoon baking powder
8 ounces (227g) unsalted butter, softened
1 egg, beaten
½ teaspoon vanilla extract
1 cup (152g) dried cranberries

Set up the Egg for 350°F (177°C) dome indirect. With the top and bottom vents wide open, light the fire and close the Egg. When the dome temperature gets up to about 250°F (121°C), about 10 minutes, close the bottom screen. When the dome temperature approaches 350°F (177°C), about 5-10 minutes, slide the top of the daisy wheel partially closed, leaving it ¼ of the way open.

In a medium bowl, mix the flour, oats, sugars, cinnamon, salt, nutmeg and baking powder until combined. With an electric mixer in a large bowl, beat the butter until smooth. Add the beaten egg and vanilla. Slowly add the dry flour mixture to the butter mixture until combined. Fold in the dried cranberries.

Drop tablespoon-sized (15ml) pieces of the batter on a greased baking pan and place on a raised rack inside the Egg. Bake at 350°F (177°C) for about 10 minutes; a little less for chewy cookies or a little longer for crispy cookies. Remove to a rack and let cool for 5 minutes before eating.

COUSIN KAREN'S SOFT PRETZELS

This recipe is from my cousin Karen Goodman Jacobson. If you have been cooking on the Egg and you have a lull in the activities, why not bake some pretzels? They don't take long, and they are a special treat warm, right off the Egg. The Egg will add a hint of smoky flavor. They are great alone, but you can try them with honey mustard as a dipping sauce or drizzle.

MAKES 6 TO 12 PRETZELS, DEPENDING UPON SIZE

1 (.25-oz [7g]) package active dry yeast

2 tablespoons (26g) brown sugar

1⅛ teaspoon (6g) salt

1½ cups (375ml) warm water (110°F [44°C])

2½ to 3 cups (312 to 375g) all-purpose flour

1 cup (90g) bread flour

2 cups (475ml) warm water

2 tablespoons (26g) baking soda

2 tablespoons (30ml) butter, melted

2 tablespoons (30g) kosher salt

Garlic salt (optional)

Cinnamon sugar (optional)

Honey mustard for dipping (optional) (We like Jack Daniel's® Honey Dijon)

In a large mixing bowl, dissolve the yeast, brown sugar and salt in 1½ cups (375ml) warm water. Stir in the flours. Knead the dough on a floured surface until smooth and elastic, about 8 minutes. Alternately, you can combine them in a stand mixer and knead, using the dough hook, for 8 minutes. Place dough in a greased bowl and turn to coat all surfaces. Cover and let rise for 1 hour.

Combine 2 cups (475ml) of warm water and the baking soda in an 8-inch (20-cm) square pan. After the dough has risen, cut it into 12 pieces. Roll each piece into a 3-foot (90-cm) rope, pencil thin or thinner. Twist into a pretzel shape and dip into the baking soda solution. To make pretzel bites, you can form into bite-size pieces and dip in baking soda solution. Place on cookie sheets sprayed with cooking spray and let rise 15 to 20 minutes.

Set the Egg for 450°F (232°C) dome indirect. With the top and bottom vents wide open, light the fire and close the Egg. When the Dome temperature gets up to about 250°F (121°C), about 10 minutes, close the bottom screen. When the dome temperature approaches 450°F (232°C), about 10 minutes, slide the top of the daisy wheel partially closed, leaving it halfway open.

Bake the pretzels for 8 to 10 minutes or until golden brown. Brush with melted butter and sprinkle with coarse salt, garlic salt or cinnamon sugar.

Note: Always burp the Egg when opening, especially when cooking over 400°F (204°C), to prevent flashback. See Chapter 1 on safety.

CHAPTER 6

WET AND DRY

CURING MEAT AND SMOKING ON THE BIG GREEN EGG

What's big, green and looks like an egg? A smokehouse, of course!

The more you use the Big Green Egg, the more you'll want to try new things. Smoking cured meat is one of those new things. You cure meat using dry or wet curing methods. For dry curing, you apply a dry rub containing curing agents to the raw meat surface. You wrap the meat in plastic wrap and either vacuum seal it or put it in large, resealable plastic bags and refrigerate it for several days, turning and massaging daily. Wet cure means "water and a curing agent." Wet curing is the process of submerging the meat for several days in a refrigerated brine containing curing agents. A brine by itself does not cure, but it adds flavors and helps the meat retain moisture. With a cure brine, the meat is cured and flavored at the same time.

After curing, meat can be refrigerated or frozen until you're ready to cook. Alternately, it can be smoked to add flavor; and, if desired, smoked to the internal temperature of fully cooked meat. In cold smoking, you smoke the meat or cheese for a few hours, but you never let it get to an internal temperature over 100°F (38°C). Cold-smoked meat is not fully cooked and therefore needs to be refrigerated or frozen until ready to cook. In hot smoking, you smoke the meat for several hours at a higher temperature until the internal temperature reaches about 160°F (71°C). Hot-smoked meat is fully cooked.

The setup I use for cold smoking utilizes an empty firebox and the A-Maze-N Pellet smoker (see Resources, page 214), which is a perforated maze that holds food-grade smoking pellets. I want to keep the meat or cheese temperature below 90°F (32°C) internal, so I use only smoke, no charcoal. I set up the Egg for direct cooking because there is no flame and I want the smoke to circulate around all the food.

HOMEMADE BACON

Making your own pork belly bacon is easy to do, and you can control the flavors you add to it. You can add spices to your dry cure to make it spicier or more savory. This recipe is for sweet bacon. Fresh pork belly can be found at Asian markets, or your supermarket's meat manager may be able to order it for you. Making your own cured, smoked bacon will elevate your neighborhood culinary stature with minimal effort. You will be a bacon bigwig in no time!

MAKES ABOUT 9 SERVINGS

3 pounds (1361g) fresh skinless, boneless pork belly

3 tablespoons (45g) quick-cure salt, such as Morton's Tenderquick®

1 tablespoon (15ml) grade B maple syrup

1 tablespoon (12g) brown sugar

1 tablespoon (6g) fresh ground black pepper

Rinse the pork belly in cold water and pat dry. In a small bowl, mix the remaining ingredients together to form a paste. Rub the paste on all sides of the pork belly. Place in a resealable plastic bag or vacuum-sealed bag. Refrigerate between 36°F and 40°F (2°C and 4°C) for six days, flipping and massaging all the sides once a day. When curing is complete, remove from the bag and rinse off thoroughly, rubbing the water into the belly.

Set up the Egg for 200°F (93°C) with a drip pan. With the top and bottom vents wide open, light the fire and close the Egg. When the dome temperature gets up to about 150°F (66°C), about 5-10 minutes, close the bottom screen. When the dome temperature approaches 200°F (93°C), about 5 minutes, slide the top of the daisy wheel closed, keeping the petals slightly open. Use only a small pile of charcoal. The firebox can be one-quarter to one-third full. Add three fruitwood chunks.

Place the pork belly on a raised grid in the dome. Smoke until the internal temperature of the pork reaches 160°F (71°C), about 2 hours. When the pork belly is cooked, let it rest for about half an hour before refrigerating or freezing.

Your homemade bacon will be easier to slice after it is refrigerated. You can slice it before freezing it in bags.

SMOKED CHEESE

Smoking adds another dimension to the flavor of cheese. It is best to use hard cheese such as Gouda, Swiss, cheddar, pepper jack or Colby. The smoking woods are usually fruitwoods, and the cheese is cold smoked until it gets no hotter than 90°F (32°C). After it has smoked for an hour or two, and before it reaches 90°F (32°C) internally, it is removed from the smoker to rest for about an hour. You may be tempted to eat it right away, and you can, but it will acquire a more balanced flavor if it's wrapped in plastic wrap and refrigerated for three days. After refrigeration, it can be eaten or it can be vacuum sealed, refrigerated or frozen.

My cold-smoking setup for the Egg include an A-Maze-N Pellet smoker (see Resources, page 214). This is a perforated tray with maze for the food-grade pellets to sit in. I clear all of the charcoal out of the Egg and place the A-Maze-N pellet smoker on the cast iron fire grate. For smokier cheese, I start the fire at both ends, and it slowly burns and smokes its way through the maze. I light one end of the maze then blow out the flame.

Place one-inch (2.5-cm) pieces of cheese on a multilevel grate. Open the top vent one quarter of the way. You may decide to let the cheese smoke longer if you like more smoke flavor. Remember that the flavor will improve the longer it is refrigerated after smoking.

If you are having trouble keeping the temperature down below 90°F (32°C), place hard plastic ice packs off to the side so no condensation drips into the Maze. Obviously, if the temperature outside is 80°F (27°C), you won't get as much smoke time before the interior gets to 90°F (32°C). Try cold smoking in the evening or in the early morning before the sun comes up. You can also keep your Egg in the shade.

CANADIAN BACON

As you may know, Canadian bacon comes from the pork loin, not from the belly like American bacon. Pork loin is very lean and can be dry. Wet curing and smoking put moisture back into it, the spices season it and the smoke adds a third flavor. Canadian bacon goes well with breakfast, in a sandwich for lunch or added to some of your own smoked cheese.

MAKES ABOUT 16 SERVINGS

1 (4-pound [1814g]) boneless pork loin

1 gallon (8L) cold water, 36°F to 40°F (2°C to 4°C), divided

4 cups (965g) quick-cure salt, such as Morton's Tenderquick®

½ cup (115g) brown sugar

2 tablespoons (19g) minced garlic

¼ cup (38g) chopped onion

1 tablespoon (8g) black peppercorns

Trim the loin of most of the fat and all of the silver skin. Keep refrigerated until ready to cure. In a large, nonreactive container, add about 1 quart (1L) of the cold water and stir in all of the other ingredients until well mixed. Add the remaining cold water and mix well. Submerge the cold loin in the curing brine. If necessary, put a plate on top to keep it from floating. Brine for 24 hours, stirring once. When fully brined, wash off the loin under cold running water, then pat dry.

Set up the Egg for 200°F (93°C) indirect with a drip pan. Use only a small pile of charcoal, with the firebox one quarter to one third full. With the top and bottom vents wide open, light the fire and close the Egg. When the dome temperature gets up to about 150°F (65°C), about 5-10 minutes, close the bottom screen. When the dome temperature approaches 200°F (93°C), about 5 minutes, slide the top of the daisy wheel closed, keeping the petals slightly open.

Add 3 fruitwood chunks and place the loin on a raised grid, up in the dome. Smoke until the internal temperature of the loin reaches 160°F (71°C), about 2 hours. Let it rest for half an hour before refrigerating or freezing. To serve, slice into ⅛-inch to ¼-inch (3 to 6-mm) slices. You can also slice before freezing.

BUCKBOARD BACON

Buckboard bacon is a great way to use a boneless pork butt. It's a treat to fry up for breakfast, and awesome on a BLT. You can also add pieces to baked beans or omelets. The butt is butterflied to a uniform thickness and rubbed with a cure. Depending on the size of the butt, it will cure for about 10 days. After it is cured, it can be hot smoked. When cooled down, it can then be sliced and refrigerated or frozen until ready to use. It is less lean than ham and meatier than pork belly bacon, and it is so easy to make! The hardest part is waiting 10 days for curing, but it is more than worth the wait. The following recipe is for one pound (450g) of pork shoulder and should be adjusted to the amount you have.

MAKES ABOUT 4 SERVINGS

CURE

1 tablespoon (15g) quick-cure salt such as Morton's Tender Quick®

½ tablespoon (5g) garlic powder

½ tablespoon (3g) fresh ground black pepper

1 teaspoon (2g) allspice

1 tablespoon (15ml) maple syrup or molasses

1 pound (454g) of pork shoulder

To make the cure, mix all of the dry ingredients together, then add the maple syrup or molasses to form a paste.

Remove the fat cap from the deboned pork butt and butterfly or slice it so that it is 2 to 3 inches (5 to 7.5cm) thick. Make two separate pieces, if necessary. All cuts should be made horizontally along the length of the butt; don't slice down or vertically. When you are done, you will have what looks like 2 or 3 layers of sliced pork butt.

Rub the cure mixture all over the surface of the meat. Make additional cure mixture if necessary to cover the pork fully. Place the meat in a heavy plastic bag, or vacuum seal it, and date the bag. Place the bag in the refrigerator for 10 days for a 3-inch (7.5-cm) thick piece, turning and flipping the bag daily. The cure mixture will create liquid brine. It is best to cure longer rather than shorter, because you want the cure to go all the way through the meat.

After the bacon has cured, remove it from the bag and rinse it under water. Place it in an ice water bath for an hour.

While the bacon is bathing, set the Egg to 225°F (107°C) indirect with a drip pan. With the top and bottom vents wide open, light the fire and close the Egg. When the dome temperature gets up to about 200°F (93°C), about 5-10 minutes, close the bottom screen. When the dome temperature approaches 225°F (107°C), about 5 minutes, slide the top of the daisy wheel closed, keeping the petals ¼ open. Add 3 wood chunks of your choice; fruitwoods are the best. When the smoke is reduced and is a bluish gray, add the bacon and smoke until an internal temperature of 150° (66°C) is reached, about 30 minutes per pound.

When the bacon is cooked it can be eaten right away, but it is much easier to slice if you refrigerate it overnight.

SPICY BEEF JERKY

Brisket jerky was one of the first meats I routinely cooked on the Big Green Egg. It smelled so good as it cooked that there was seldom much left afterward! This jerky isn't true jerky because it hasn't been completely dehydrated. As an alternative to the seasoning below, the brisket can be marinated in teriyaki (page 127).

MAKES 12 SERVINGS UNLESS YOU EAT THEM ALL WHILE COOKING

4 pounds (1814g) brisket flap meat, ¼-inch (6mm) slices

2 cups (475ml) soy sauce

2 cups (475ml) Worcestershire sauce

2 tablespoons (19g) minced garlic

2 tablespoons (8g) crushed red pepper flakes

1 cup (230g) brown sugar

1 tablespoon (9g) salt

1 tablespoon (6g) fresh ground black pepper

1 (7-oz [207-ml]) can chipotle in adobo sauce, puréed

1 cup (240ml) water

Mix all ingredients together except for the brisket and chipotle. Trim all visible fat from the brisket and slice in ¼-inch (6-mm) slices with the grain. The slices can be up to 8 inches (20 cm) long. It will slice more easily if it is partially frozen. Place the marinade and slices in a 2-gallon (7.5-L) resealable freezer bag and mix well by massaging the bag to cover all the slices. Lay the bag in a large casserole dish and refrigerate for 12 to 24 hours, turning and massaging often.

Set up the Egg for 250°F (121°C) indirect with a drip pan. With the top and bottom vents wide open, light the fire and close the Egg. When the dome temperature gets up to about 200°F (93°C), about 10 minutes, close the bottom screen. When the dome temperature approaches 250°F (121°C), about 5 minutes, slide the top of the daisy wheel closed, keeping the petals halfway open. Fill the Egg with charcoal to the top of the firebox. Set two grates on top of each other, offset by 90°, to reduce the gaps in the grates. You can also use perforated or disposable grill toppers.

When the Egg is up to temperature, remove the brisket slices from the marinade. Do not dry them or shake off any marinade. Pile the slices in the center of the grate so that all of them are above the drip pan. Discard the bag with the marinade.

Every hour or so, move the jerky around with a pair of tongs. As the jerky cooks, the pieces will shrink and the pile of meat will become smaller. (Pieces will also be disappearing every time you open the Egg!) Cook it for up to 6 hours (or until all the pieces have been eaten). Store the jerky in the refrigerator for up to a week.

CHAPTER 7

DEEP FRYING, GRIDDLING AND WOK-ING AROUND

OTHER GREAT WAYS TO COOK ON THE BIG GREEN EGG

The Big Green Egg is the Ultimate Cooking Experience™ and also the most versatile cooking appliance. Sure, you can wok and deep fry in the kitchen. You know how good the food tastes. You also know you'll be reminded for days that you smelled up the house with fried oil, garlic and fish! Cook it all on the Egg and you won't heat up the house or stink it up for days.

Using a Dutch oven on the Egg is the perfect way to deep fry. It stays hot and helps the oil recover faster if the temperature drops. It is much safer than using a fry pan for shallow-frying, which I would not recommend. A Dutch oven has a bale handle and a lid, and it's deep enough to make deep-frying safe and efficient. Always add oil to the Dutch oven when it is off the Egg, and never to more than 2½ inches (6cm) from the top. Oil in a covered Dutch oven can heat up to the desired temperature of 325°F to 375°F (160°C to 190°C) while the Egg is coming up to temperature. As long as the lid is on the Dutch oven when the dome is closed, there will never be a problem with the oil catching fire. (This has never happened to me, but if it happens to you, replace the lid on the Dutch oven and close the dome and vents until the fire snuffs out.) If the oil gets too hot, cover the Dutch oven and take it off the Egg. It will then be safe to remove the lid and cool the oil.

The Big Green Egg is perfect for a wok as well. The wok temperature should be up to about 450°F (232°C), and the Egg has no difficulty getting it there! The wok sits right on the grid. All you need is a pair of welder's gloves for handling it. Wok cooking is quick, so make sure you have all your ingredients measured and available before starting. If your wok has a rounded bottom, make sure you have a wok stand or a large pot handy to keep it upright when you remove it from the Egg.

GRIDDLED CRAB CAKES

Crab cakes are a favorite in seaside locations, especially Maryland. If you aren't near fresh crabmeat sources, then canned, pasteurized lump crabmeat is readily available. You can vary the recipe to your own taste by adding minced red bell peppers, scallions or other herbs. Serving with the rémoulade sauce is good, but simple fresh-squeezed lemon on your crispy, browned crab cake might just float your boat!

MAKES ABOUT 6 SERVINGS

1 cup (121g) bread crumbs, divided
4 tablespoons (59ml) mayonnaise
2 tablespoons (30ml) whole-grain Dijon mustard
2 tablespoons (30ml) lemon juice
⅓ cup (50g) minced red onion
1 tablespoon (3g) chopped parsley
1 teaspoon (5g) sea salt
½ teaspoon black pepper
¼ teaspoon cayenne pepper
1 pound (454g) lump crabmeat
3 tablespoons (45ml) olive oil
Rémoulade sauce

Combine half of the breadcrumbs with the mayonnaise, mustard, lemon juice, red onion, chopped parsley, salt and peppers in a bowl until well mixed. Pick through the crabmeat and discard any shells or cartilage. Gently mix the crabmeat into the bowl with the other ingredients, being careful not to break up the crab pieces too much. Taste and add more spice if desired. Make eight ⅓-cup (75-ml) patties and gently pat them to ½ inch (1.5 cm) thickness. On a flat surface, coat the patties with the remaining bread crumbs and refrigerate for half an hour.

Set the Egg for 350°F (177°C) direct, and use either the half-round cast iron griddle grate or a cast iron fry pan that will fit on your Egg, including the handle. With the top and bottom vents wide open, light the fire and close the Egg. When the dome temperature gets up to about 250°F (121°C), about 10 minutes, close the bottom screen. When the dome temperature approaches 350°F (177°C), about 5-10 minutes, slide the top of the daisy wheel partially closed, leaving it ¼ of the way open.

Add olive oil to coat the bottom of the griddle or pan. When it's hot, add the crab cakes. Cook for 3 to 4 minutes per side, turning once with a spatula, until golden brown. Remove to a rack to drain before serving. Serve with rémoulade on the side.

SEARED AND SAUCED SEA SCALLOPS

When cooked correctly, scallops are sweet, juicy and tender. When overcooked, they are dry and chewy. Sea scallops are much larger than bay scallops, and they cost more. This recipe calls for sea scallops, but bay scallops can be substituted because we are not cooking on a grill grid grate, but in a pan, so they won't fall through. Dry scallops are not treated with preservatives. They are creamy and slightly pink in color. Wet scallops have been treated and do not sear as well because they have retained liquid. Their color is very bright white. I think dry sea scallops taste much better than wet. Frozen scallops are often frozen at sea, so preservatives are not necessary. Any fresh scallop should smell sweet and have an ocean smell, not a fishy smell. For a variation on the sauce recipe, fry some bacon before sautéing the onion and garlic and crumble it into the sauce.

MAKES ABOUT 4 SERVINGS

12 large sea scallops
¼ cup (60ml) olive oil, divided
Salt and pepper

SAUCE
4 shallots, finely diced
1 clove garlic, minced
2 tablespoons (30g) unsalted butter
¼ cup (60ml) apple cider vinegar
1 tablespoon (15ml) lemon juice
1 teaspoon (4g) sugar
1 tablespoon (3g) chopped fresh parsley

Rinse the scallops and remove the abductor muscle on the side. Pat dry, coat with olive oil and sprinkle with salt and pepper.

Set the Egg for 350°F (177°C) direct and use either the half-round cast iron griddle grate or a cast iron fry pan that fits in the Egg, including the handle. With the top and bottom vents wide open, light the fire and close the Egg. When the dome temperature gets up to about 250°F (121°C), about 5 minutes, close the bottom screen. When the dome temperature approaches 350°F (177°C), about 5-10 minutes, slide the top of the daisy wheel partially closed, leaving it ¼ of the way open.

Add olive oil to coat the bottom of the griddle or pan. When it's hot, add the scallops. Sear for 2 to 3 minutes until browned, flip and cook for an additional 2 minutes. Cook until the insides are still soft and have a slightly opaque appearance. They should not be white! You can cook the first scallop and check for doneness before the others to get your sea legs under you. If they are chewy, they are overcooked.

After the scallops have cooled, pour a little more olive oil into the griddle or fry pan. Add the shallots and sauté for about 3 minutes until soft. Add the garlic and cook for another minute. If using a griddle, in a separate saucepan, melt the butter and add the vinegar, lemon juice and sugar. Add the sautéed garlic and shallots to the pan and simmer for about a minute. If you are using a frying pan, you won't need a saucepan because the butter, vinegar and lemon juice can be added directly to the frying pan. Remove from the heat and add the chopped parsley. Serve the sauce over the scallops.

THE BEST BEEF BRISKET HASH

Brisket hash is my way of using leftover brisket similar to a traditional corned beef or ham boiled dinner hash. Traditionally, after we let the boiled dinner cook for several hours, it's ready to eat. The next day, we chop it up and sauté it into a hash. A key to the hash flavor is that all of the vegetables are cooked in the meat juices, or "liquor." At hunting camp, there is a hand-written note on the wall on the back of the stove that Uncle Sid wrote 60 years ago. It states to not throw out the "pot liquor," but to reserve it. In my recipe, cooking the vegetables in beef broth is my way of making pot liquor.

MAKES ABOUT 6 SERVINGS

4 cups (900g) chopped barbecued beef brisket

3 cups (750ml) beef broth

3 large potatoes

2 onions

½ turnip

3 parsnips

4 carrots

½ head green cabbage

2 cups (475ml) pot liquor

3 tablespoons (45ml) apple cider vinegar

3 tablespoons (45ml) brown mustard

2 teaspoons (6g) garlic powder

1 teaspoon (5g) salt

½ teaspoon black pepper

4 tablespoons (60ml) vegetable oil

Additional mustard or ketchup (optional)

Poached eggs (optional)

Cut all the vegetables into ½-inch (1.5-cm) cubes or pieces and boil in the beef broth until tender, 25 to 30 minutes. Remove from the heat and cooking broth, reserving broth, and refrigerate for 12 hours, or overnight. Chop the brisket into ½-inch (1.5-cm) cubes or pieces and add to the drained vegetables. Add the reserved pot liquor, vinegar, mustard and spices and mix. Press the mixture into patties, or leave as is for hash.

Set the Egg for 350°F (177°C) direct, and use either the half-round cast iron griddle grate or a cast iron fry pan that will fit on the Egg, including the handle. With the top and bottom vents wide open, light the fire and close the Egg. When the dome temperature gets up to about 250°F (121°C), about 10 minutes, close the bottom screen. When the dome temperature approaches 350°F (177°C), about 5-10 minutes, slide the top of the daisy wheel partially closed, leaving it ¼ of the way open.

Add vegetable oil to coat the bottom of the griddle or pan and when hot, add the hash or patties. Cook until browned on the bottom, about 5 minutes, then flip and cook for another 4 minutes. When done, serve with mustard, ketchup or a poached egg on top.

SULLY'S DAMN DIP

This recipe was contributed by Mike "Sully" Sullivan. Sully sometimes made this spicy late-night dip at competitions, and it grew in popularity until people started expecting it at every competition. It is so popular that, even when he was planning to make it, people still asked him, "Hey, Sully, are you making dip tonight?" His reply became, "All right! I'll make the damn dip!" The dip is different every time he makes it; I am giving the basic recipe for you to change as you see fit. It will still be the best damn dip you ever had! One of the best things about it is that you can pick up ingredients on your way to a party or barbecue and put it together when you get there! All of the quantities are based on using a 17-inch (42.5-cm) cast iron pan. This pan has no handle, and it fits on the XL Big Green Egg. The Damn Dip can be halved and cooked in a Dutch oven if you don't have a cast iron pan without a handle, but you won't get to enjoy as much of it!

MAKES ABOUT 24 SERVINGS

6 cans hot chili with beans, such as Hormel®

Several dashes hot sauce (Sully's favorite is Dirty Dick's®)

48 ounces (1361g) cream cheese (Sully prefers Philly Cream Cheese®)

12 oz (360g) each of three kinds of salsa (Sully always includes Mrs. Renfro's Green Chili Salsa®; sweet salsa with some heat works well)

8 to 12 oz (277 to 340g) mixed mild shredded cheeses such as mozzarella, cheddar and provolone

Tortilla chips for serving

Pour the canned chili into the cast iron pan. Add several dashes of hot sauce. Cube the cream cheese into 1-inch (2.5-cm) pieces and place over the chili in the pan. Pour the salsas over the chili and cream cheese. Layer the cheeses on top of the salsa. You can add sliced peppers or more hot sauce to this layer.

Set the Egg at 350°F (177°C) dome indirect. With the top and bottom vents wide open, light the fire and close the Egg. When the dome temperature gets up to about 250°F (121°C), about 10 minutes, close the bottom screen. When the dome temperature approaches 350°F (177°C), about 5-10 minutes, slide the top of the daisy wheel partially closed, leaving it ¼ of the way open.

When the fire is up to temperature, put the pan on the grate. Cook the Damn Dip, rotating often, until it is bubbly all over and the shredded cheese is melted to a liquid goo.

Serve with a hefty tortilla chip. The only rule of Damn Dip is no stirring allowed, EVAH!!!

DEEP-FRIED CATFISH

Catfish is very sweet. When it's deep-fried, you encounter a crispy, crunchy coating and a sweet, soft filet that will make you smile. Farm-raising catfish has made frozen catfish readily available. I've never fished for catfish, but I've often caught their smaller cousin, horn pout. My father and I used to go "poutin'" on Lake Umbagog on the New Hampshire-Maine border. We fished at night down near the bottom. They were not very large—only 6 to 8 inches (15 to 20cm)—but just as sweet and tasty as catfish.

MAKES ABOUT 6 SERVINGS

6 skinless catfish fillets

Oil for frying

3 cups (511g) cornmeal

1 teaspoon (8g) garlic powder

1 teaspoon (8g) onion powder

1 tablespoon (15g) salt

1 tablespoon (15g) coarse-ground pepper

1½ cups (375ml) buttermilk

Set up the Egg for 400°F (204°C) indirect. With the top and bottom vents wide open, light the fire and close the Egg. When the dome temperature gets up to about 250°F (121°C), about 10 minutes, close the bottom screen. When the dome temperature approaches 400°F (204°C), about 10 minutes, slide the top of the daisy wheel partially closed, keeping it ¼ open.

Off the fire, put about 2 inches (5cm) of oil in the Dutch oven, cover and place on the Egg. Close the dome on the Egg and prepare the catfish while the oil is getting hot. Never close the dome when the cover is off of the Dutch oven.

In a deep pie plate or a small casserole dish, mix together all of the dry ingredients. Rinse the catfish and pat dry. Dust the fillets with the dry mix, and then dredge them in the buttermilk. Press each fillet into the dry mix to coat, then repeat on the second side.

Set the breaded catfish on a rack until the oil is hot, 350°F (177°C). Cook fillets for 2 to 3 minutes on each side in the hot oil. The coating should be crunchy and the fish should be cooked to 150°F (75°C). Let the cooked fish drain on a rack until all fillets are cooked. Serve with tartar sauce or in a Po' Boy sandwich (page 65).

CINDI'S DEEP-FRIED COCONUT SHRIMP

Nothing tastes better than deep-fried shellfish, and this sweet and crunchy shrimp will definitely satisfy. Shelled, deveined and breaded shrimp cooks quickly and perfectly every time. Accompanied by a sweet and spicy dipping sauce, it will please any group gathering around your Egg!

MAKES ABOUT 4 SERVINGS

1 pound (454g) medium to large fresh or frozen shrimp

½ cup (60g) cornstarch

2 eggs

1 cup (240ml) piña colada mix such as Mr. & Mrs. T's®

1 cup (60g) panko breadcrumbs

1 cup (76g) sweetened shredded coconut

Oil for deep-frying

1 jar spicy chutney, puréed

Rinse shrimp in a colander under cold water, then place them on a paper towel-lined baking sheet and pat them dry. Put the cornstarch in a resealable bag. In a shallow bowl or pie plate, thoroughly combine the eggs with the piña colada mix. In a separate resealable bag, mix the breadcrumbs and shredded coconut. Place the shrimp, 4 or 5 at a time, into the cornstarch, remove and place in the egg wash, then shake them in the breadcrumb mixture. Remove from the bag and place on a paper-towel-lined baking sheet on a drying rack until all are coated.

Set the Egg for 400°F (204°C) direct. With the top and bottom vents wide open, light the fire and close the Egg. When the dome temperature gets up to about 250°F (121°C), about 10 minutes, close the bottom screen. When the dome temperature approaches 400°F (204°C), about 10 minutes, slide the top of the daisy wheel partially closed, keeping it ¼ open.

Off the fire, put about 4 inches (10 cm) of oil in the Dutch oven, cover and place on the Egg. Close the dome and heat until the oil reaches 375°F (191°C). Open the Egg and take the cover off of the Dutch oven. Never close the dome when the cover is off of the Dutch oven. Carefully drop a few shrimp at a time into the hot oil and cook until golden, about 3 to 4 minutes, being careful not to burn them. Remove with a slotted spoon to a drying rack until all are cooked.

Serve warm with the chutney sauce for dipping.

SPICY, CORNY BACON FRITTERS

I think fritters are a good excuse to eat something deep-fried! I like to munch on them with a meal, as an appetizer, or just while hanging around the Egg. I have increased that urge by adding bacon and jalapeños. They are crunchy on the outside, soft on the inside and studded with corn, bacon and peppers. Your favorite rub sprinkled on the finished fritter is a great addition. If you need even more flavor, drizzle them with honey mustard.

MAKES ABOUT 6 SERVINGS

4 slices of thick-cut bacon

½ cup (62g) all-purpose flour

1 cup (170g) cornmeal

½ teaspoon baking powder

½ teaspoon salt

½ teaspoon pepper

2 teaspoons (4g) cayenne pepper

1 large egg, beaten

1 cup (240ml) whole milk or buttermilk

1 tablespoon (15g) bacon fat or butter

1 jalapeño pepper, seeded, ribs removed and diced

½ cup (120g) fresh corn or thawed, frozen kernels

2 quarts (2L) vegetable oil for frying

Set up the egg for 400°F (204°C) indirect. With the top and bottom vents wide open, light the fire and close the Egg. When the dome temperature gets up to about 250°F (121°C), about 10 minutes, close the bottom screen. When the dome temperature approaches 400°F (204°C), about 10 minutes, slide the top of the daisy wheel partially closed, keeping it ¼ open.

Grill the bacon in a Dutch oven until it is crisp. Remove the bacon and crumble to small pieces the size of a kernel of corn. Reserve about 1 tablespoon (15ml) of the rendered bacon fat for the batter. With the Dutch oven away from the fire, add the oil for frying, 2 inches (5cm) deep. Cover the Dutch oven and place it back on the 400°F (204°C) Egg, then close the dome. Never close the dome when the cover is off of the Dutch oven. Make the batter while the oil heats to 360°F (182°C).

In a large bowl, combine the flour, cornmeal, baking powder, salt and peppers and stir until well blended. In a small bowl, combine the egg, milk, bacon fat, jalapeño, corn and crumbled bacon. When blended, stir wet ingredients into dry until the batter is well blended, the consistency of mashed potatoes. If it's too stiff, add a little more milk.

When the oil temperature reaches 360°F (182°C), start frying the fritters, about 1 rounded tablespoon (15ml) each. Cook until golden brown, flipping once, about 4 minutes total. The temperature of the oil may drop a bit when the fritters are added. This is normal, and the oil temperature should recover. If the oil gets below 300°F (150°C), put the Dutch oven cover back on, close the Egg and let the temperature rise again. If the oil gets above 400°F (204°C), put the lid back on the Dutch oven and remove it from the Egg for a few minutes. Adjust the vents in the Egg to increase or decrease the Egg temperature.

When the fritters are done, place them on a drying rack and sprinkle with your favorite spice rub. Fry the fritters in batches until all the batter is finished. Serve warm.

SCOTCH EGGS

Scotch eggs come from across the pond and are a tasty treat from morning to night, from breakfast until the bars close. I like hard-boiled eggs, but wrapping them in sausage and deep frying them makes my heart skip a beat. (Hopefully, only one!) Use any flavor of sausage, or make your own. You can also experiment with boiling the eggs a little less so they are soft-boiled but cooked enough to hold together when you remove their shells. You can also bake Scotch eggs, indirectly, in the Egg instead of deep-frying them, to achieve a smoky flavor.

MAKES ABOUT 6 SERVINGS

1 pound (454g) sausage

6 eggs, hard-boiled, cooled and shells removed

1 beaten egg

½ cup (30g) dry breadcrumbs

1 quart (1L) vegetable oil for frying

Separate the sausage into 6 equal parts and press each piece into a 4-inch (10-cm) circle. Place one hard-boiled egg in the center of each sausage patty and wrap the sausage around the egg, sealing completely. Roll each wrapped egg in the beaten egg and then roll in the breadcrumbs to coat.

Set up the Egg for 400°F (204°C) dome direct. With the top and bottom vents wide open, light the fire and close the Egg. When the dome temperature gets up to about 250°F (121°C), about 10 minutes, close the bottom screen. When the dome temperature approaches 400°F (204°C), about 10 minutes, slide the top of the daisy wheel partially closed, keeping it ¼ open.

Add the oil to a Dutch oven, about 4 inches (10 cm) deep; cover and heat on the Egg, dome closed, until the oil reaches 375°F (191°C). Never close the dome when the cover is off of the Dutch oven. Being careful not to overcrowd the pan, place the eggs, a couple at a time, into the hot oil and fry for about 4 minutes, until the temperature of the sausage reaches 165°F (74°C). Remove from the oil and place on a rack. Sprinkle with your favorite rub and cool for 5 minutes. Scotch eggs can be eaten hot or cold. Try cutting them up and putting them on your salad!

SPICY FRIED CHICKEN

Chicken can be successfully cooked in so many ways. Deep-frying, however, gives such a juicy and crispy bite that it is my favorite. Some of the best fried chicken I have ever had was in Nashville, Tennessee on our way to the Jack Daniel's Invitational World Barbecue Championship. It was at Prince's Hot Chicken Shack. Very hot, very good! This recipe has just a little heat from the cayenne pepper. For more of a kick, add smoked paprika and more cayenne.

MAKES 6 TO 8 SERVINGS

3 pounds (1350g) chicken pieces
2 tablespoons (30g) kosher salt, divided
2 cups (474ml) buttermilk
3 cups (375g) all purpose flour
1 tablespoon (6g) black pepper
1 teaspoon (2g) cayenne pepper
1 tablespoon (9g) garlic powder
1 tablespoon (9g) onion powder
Oil for frying

In a large bowl, add half of the salt to the buttermilk and mix well. Add the chicken pieces, coat well, cover and refrigerate for 2 to 8 hours.

Set the Egg for 400°F (204°C) indirect. With the top and bottom vents wide open, light the fire and close the Egg. When the dome temperature gets up to about 250°F (121°C), about 10 minutes, close the bottom screen. When the dome temperature approaches 400°F (204°C), about 10 minutes, slide the top of the daisy wheel partially closed, keeping it ¼ open.

Off the fire, put about 3 inches (7.5 cm) of oil in a Dutch oven, cover and place on the Egg, then close the dome. Never close the dome when the cover is off of the Dutch oven.

Prepare the flour mixture while the oil is heating. In a pie plate or a small casserole dish, mix together the flour, remaining salt, black pepper, cayenne pepper, garlic powder and onion powder. Remove the chicken pieces from the buttermilk and let the excess drip off. Place each piece in the flour mixture to coat, then place on a rack for 10 minutes.

When the oil reaches between 350°F and 375°F (177°C and 190°C), fry the chicken pieces, being careful not to overcrowd the Dutch oven. Cook until the chicken is crisp and its internal temperature is at least 165°F (74°C), about 8–10 minutes each side. Remove from the oil to a cooling rack. Repeat until the remaining chicken is cooked.

We must learn to reawaken and keep ourselves awake, not by mechanical means, but by an infinite expectation of the dawn.

DEEP-FRIED BRISKET EMPANADAS

Brisket empanadas are a great way to serve leftover barbecued beef brisket. The outsides are crisp and the insides are beefy, sweet and juicy. The French fried onions add a different crunch of flavor to the mix. Instead of deep-frying the empanadas, you can coat them with an egg wash or cooking spray and bake them.

MAKES 12 EMPANADAS

1 pound (454g) cooked barbecued beef brisket, chopped, with barbecue sauce

12 frozen pastry rounds such as Goya Discos™ (you may substitute egg roll wrappers or pie dough), thawed

2 cups (116g) French fried onions

4 cups (1L) vegetable oil for frying

Set the Egg for 400°F (204°C) direct. With the top and bottom vents wide open, light the fire and close the Egg. When the dome temperature gets up to about 250°F (121°C), about 10 minutes, close the bottom screen. When the dome temperature approaches 400°F (204°C), about 10 minutes, slide the top of the daisy wheel partially closed, keeping it ¼ open. Add the oil to a Dutch oven, about 2 inches (5 cm) deep. Cover, place Dutch oven on the Egg and then close the dome. Heat on the Egg until the oil reaches 375°F (191°C). Never close the dome when the cover is off of the Dutch oven.

While the oil is heating, place a heaping tablespoon of brisket on a pastry round. Add a good pinch of French fried onions on top, then wet your finger in water and fold the filled disco in half. Press to seal. A dough press works well, but always remember to wet the edges before pressing the dough closed.

When the oil is hot, gently add 4 folded empanadas to the oil and fry, flipping once, for 5 to 6 minutes, or until golden brown and crisp. Remove to a drying rack and repeat until finished.

DOUBLE CRUNCH FRIED PICKLES

Fried pickles are not complicated. They're just pickles...or so you thought! What kind of pickle do you want to fry? Sweet or sour? Spears or chips? Served with mustard or ketchup? Have a pickle fry-off and let your friends and family decide! I prefer sweet cucumber chips, but that's just me. The cornmeal in the batter adds an extra crunch. For an extra treat, if dill pickles are your preference, try kosher dill pickles. They are garlicky and full of flavor.

MAKES ABOUT 4 SERVINGS

1 cup (120g) all-purpose flour

1 cup (170g) cornmeal

1 teaspoon (3g) garlic powder

1 teaspoon (3g) onion powder

1 teaspoon (2g) ground black pepper

2 cup (475ml) buttermilk

1 cup (150g) sliced pickle chips, sweet or dill

1 quart (1L) vegetable oil for frying

Salt

Set the Egg at 400°F (204°C) indirect. With the top and bottom vents wide open, light the fire and close the Egg. When the dome temperature gets up to about 250°F (121°C), about 10 minutes, close the bottom screen. When the dome temperature approaches 400°F (204°C), about 10 minutes, slide the top of the daisy wheel partially closed, keeping it ¼ open.

Off of the fire, add oil to a Dutch oven, 2 inches (5 cm) deep. Cover it and place it on the Egg, then close the dome. Never close the dome when the cover is off of the Dutch oven.

Prepare the pickles while the oil heats to 350°F. In a large bowl, mix all of the dry ingredients. Add the buttermilk and mix by hand until well blended. Pat the pickle chips dry.

When the oil reaches a temperature of around 350°F (177°C), add several chips to the buttermilk mixture to coat, and gently slip them into the hot oil. Cook for 2 to 3 minutes, flipping once, until they are golden brown. Remove to a rack and dust with salt. Repeat until all pickles are cooked. Serve with mustard, ketchup, or your favorite dipping sauce.

"HONEY JACK" APPLE NACHOS

These nachos are a great crowd-pleaser. Apple pie, fresh cinnamon-sugar tortilla chips and homemade whipped cream are a delicious combination of sweet and tart with contrasting textures from crisp to creamy. The cinnamon-sugar chips are very crisp and are superb by themselves.

MAKES ABOUT 10 SERVINGS

APPLE FILLING

10 to 12 firm apples

¼ cup (57g) butter

1 teaspoon (3g) salt

1 teaspoon (2g) cinnamon

¾ teaspoon nutmeg

2 ounces (60ml) honey whiskey such as Jack Daniel's Tennessee Honey Whiskey™ (alcohol will cook off)

Juice of 1 lemon

¼ cup (60ml) maple syrup

½ cup (100g) dark brown sugar

1 tablespoon (8g) flour

CINNAMON TORTILLA CHIPS

8 flour tortillas, cut into 8 triangles

1 to 2 cups (200 to 400g) cinnamon sugar

Oil for frying

WHIPPED CREAM TOPPING

1¼ cups (295ml) heavy cream

2 tablespoons (30ml) maple syrup

2 tablespoons (30ml) Jack Daniel's Honey Liqueur™ (alcohol will NOT cook off)

To make the apple filling, peel, core and chop the apples. Heat pan on stove over medium-high heat and add butter. When the butter is melted, reduce the heat to medium and add the apples and seasonings. Sauté until the apples begin to soften. Remove from heat and add whiskey. Return to heat and add lemon juice, maple syrup and brown sugar. Cook until the sugar dissolves. Sprinkle with the flour, stir and cook until thickened. Strain mixture, reserving liquid. Refrigerate liquid.

Next, fry the chips. With the top and bottom vents wide open, light the fire and close the Egg. When the dome temperature gets up to about 250°F (121°C), about 10 minutes, close the bottom screen. When the dome temperature approaches 400°F (204°C), about 10 minutes, slide the top of the daisy wheel partially closed, keeping it ¼ open.

Away from the Egg, add 2 inches (10 cm) of oil to the Dutch oven, cover, put on the Egg and close the dome. Heat oil to 350°F (177°C) with the lid on the Dutch oven and the dome closed. Never close the dome when the cover is off of the Dutch oven.

When the oil is up to temperature, fry the tortilla chips with the dome open, cooking both sides, about one minute per side. Remove to a rack to cool. When cool enough to handle, toss into the cinnamon sugar, coating both sides.

Make the whipped cream while the chips cool. In a cold bowl, beat the cream, syrup and whiskey until stiff peaks form. To assemble, top the chips with the apple mixture. Drizzle the cold reserved liquid over the filling and add dollops of whipped cream.

UNASSUMING FRIED PLANTAINS

Plantains are the banana's first cousin once removed. Their shape is similar to that of bananas, but they are starchy like potatoes. As plantains ripen, they turn color from green to yellow to black. For this recipe, use green plantains because they are firmest and will be crispy when fried. As an alternative, try yellow plantains. Being softer than the green plantains, they should be sliced twice as thick and baked on the Egg. Smash the slices to ½ inch (1.5 cm) when partially cooked, then return to the Egg to crisp. Fried plantains are great for snacking, for entertaining or as a garnish to your meal.

MAKES ABOUT 6 SERVINGS

2 green plantains, sliced into ¾-inch (1.9-cm) pieces
1 quart (1L) vegetable oil for frying
Salt or your favorite rub

Set up the Egg for 400° (204°C) direct. With the top and bottom vents wide open, light the fire and close the Egg. When the dome temperature gets up to about 250°F (121°C), about 10 minutes, close the bottom screen. When the dome temperature approaches 400°F (204°C), about 10 minutes, slide the top of the daisy wheel partially closed, keeping it ¼ open.

Away from the Egg, add the oil to a Dutch oven, about 4 inches (10 cm) deep. Cover it and heat on the Egg until the oil reaches 350°F (177°C). Never close the dome when the cover is off of the Dutch oven.

When the oil is hot, remove the cover and fry the slices in the hot oil for about 6 minutes; remove and let drain on a rack. When they are cool enough to handle, flatten the slices with the heel of your palm to about a ¼-inch (6-mm) thickness. Re-fry the slices until they are browned and crisp, about 3 minutes more. Remove from the oil to a rack to drain, sprinkle with salt or your favorite rub and serve!

PORK CRACKLIN'S

Pork cracklin's are deep-fried pork belly skin. A lot of fat renders out during cooking, leaving a crunchy, creamy and salty snack. They can be left at room temperature for a few days, but they don't usually last that long. You can use the skin from the pork belly left over from bacon or the grilled Asian pork belly, or from salt pork. Nothing goes to waste!

MAKES ABOUT 3 SERVINGS

1 pound (454g) pork belly skin
2 cups (475ml) vegetable oil for frying
Salt to taste

Slice the pork skin into ¾ by 1-inch (2 by 2.5-cm) pieces and pat dry. Set the Egg for 400°F (204°C) dome direct. With the top and bottom vents wide open, light the fire and close the Egg. When the dome temperature gets up to about 250°F (121°C), about 10 minutes, close the bottom screen. When the dome temperature approaches 400°F (204°C), about 10 minutes, slide the top of the daisy wheel partially closed, keeping it ¼ open.

Off of the fire, add the vegetable oil to the Dutch oven, cover and heat to 325°F (163°C) with the dome closed. Never close the dome when the cover is off of the Dutch oven.

When the oil is hot, remove the cover and carefully add a dozen or so skin pieces to the oil. Fry for 20 to 25 minutes, turning occasionally until they float. They should be dark and crispy. Remove them from the Dutch oven, season with salt, and let them drain on a rack. As you cook the skin in batches, make sure the oil temperature stays around 325°F (163°C).

STIR-FRIED BRUSSELS SPROUTS WITH BACON

I like brussels sprouts. To get our kids to eat them, I told them they were baby cabbages. When boiled, they can be bitter and mushy. Stir-fried in bacon fat, however, they are crispy, and the bacon accents their unique taste. If everything we ate were sweet, it would get boring. However, bacon is always invited to the table.

MAKES ABOUT 4 SERVINGS

½ pound (225g) thick-cut maple bacon, diced

1 pound (454g) brussels sprouts

¼ cup (40g) sliced shallots

2 tablespoons (19g) chopped garlic

1 tablespoon (15ml) olive oil

¼ teaspoon salt

¼ teaspoon black pepper

Set up the Egg for 500°F (260°C) direct. With the top and bottom vents wide open, light the fire and close the Egg. When the dome temperature gets up to about 250°F (121°C), about 10 minutes, close the bottom screen. When the dome temperature approaches 500°F (260°C), about 10 minutes, slide the top of the daisy wheel partially closed, keeping it halfway open.

While the Egg is heating up, dice the bacon into ⅜-inch (9-mm) cubes. Cut off the bottoms of the brussels sprouts cores and remove any dry leaves. Cut the sprouts in half, slicing through their cores. Slice the shallots and chop the garlic.

Place the wok on the Egg when the fire is hot. When a drop of water dances on the wok surface, add the olive oil and the diced bacon. Stir the bacon until lightly browned, about 3 minutes, then add the shallots and garlic. Cook and stir for another 3 minutes. Add the halved brussels sprouts, the salt and the pepper, and stir-fry for 8 to 10 minutes, until they are browned on the outside. Remove and serve.

STIR-FRY SUMMER SUCCOTASH

I love this summer succotash recipe because it uses fresh corn, green beans, bacon and salt pork! The other vegetables and spices make this a very colorful and delicious side dish. The corn and green beans are cooked but still crisp for a very fresh taste. As an alternative, you can make winter succotash with frozen corn and frozen lima beans instead of the green beans. With the bacon, salt pork and other spices, you can't go wrong either way!

MAKES ABOUT 8 SERVINGS

¼ pound (120g) bacon, sliced

¼ pound (120g) salt pork, rind removed, sliced and chopped

¾ cup (114g) chopped onion

2 tablespoons (19g) minced garlic

¾ cup (128g) red sweet pepper

6 ears fresh corn on the cob

1½ cups (225g) fresh green beans, chopped into 1-inch (2.5-cm) pieces

1 teaspoon (6g) salt

1 teaspoon (1g) pepper

4 tablespoons (60g) butter

½ teaspoon dried thyme

½ teaspoon cayenne pepper

¼ cup (12g) chopped scallions, green and white pieces

1 tablespoon (3g) fresh basil, chopped

Set the Egg for 450°F (230°C) direct. With the top and bottom vents wide open, light the fire and close the Egg. When the dome temperature gets up to about 250°F (121°C), about 10 minutes, close the bottom screen. When the dome temperature approaches 450°F (232°C), about 10 minutes, slide the top of the daisy wheel partially closed, keeping it halfway open.

Set the wok on the grate and heat until a drop of water dances on the bottom. Add the chopped bacon and salt pork and stir-fry until cooked, with fat rendered but not completely crisp. Add onions and garlic and stir-fry for 3 minutes, until the onion is translucent, but not browned. Add the red pepper, corn, green beans, salt, pepper, butter, thyme and cayenne pepper and stir-fry until the green beans are a vivid green and all the vegetables have softened, but are still crisp, about 5 minutes. Add the scallions and basil, stir thoroughly, remove from the heat and serve.

STIR-FRIED GARLIC PORK WITH CUCUMBER

Stir-frying is not very difficult; you just need to have all of your ingredients ready to use. The first time might seem hectic, but with very little practice, you will be stir-frying, bing, bang, boom! In this recipe, coating the pork in cornstarch is called velveting. It keeps the meat moist as it cooks. You will taste the pork with the sweet, savory and salty sauce coating, slightly crisp red peppers, and delicious cucumber served "al dente." This dish tastes great and is fun to make!

MAKES ABOUT 6 SERVINGS

1 pound (454g) boneless country-style ribs from the blade end of the loin; or lean, boneless pork shoulder

1 tablespoon (10g) cornstarch

1 tablespoon (15ml) mirin or rice wine

1 tablespoon (13g) brown sugar

2 tablespoons (30ml) soy sauce

1 tablespoon (15ml) Worcestershire sauce

½ teaspoon salt

¼ cup (60ml) low sodium chicken broth

4 tablespoons (60ml) vegetable oil, divided

1 red pepper, stemmed, seeded, deveined and chopped

4 tablespoons (38g) chopped garlic

2 tablespoons (19g) chopped ginger

1 large English (seedless) cucumber, sliced on the diagonal, ¼ inch (6mm) thick

Sliced green onions for garnish

Slice the pork into 1-inch (2.5-cm) long and ¼-inch (6-mm) thick slices. In a medium bowl, mix the cornstarch with the mirin, and add the sliced pork to coat. In a separate bowl, add the sugar, soy sauce, Worcestershire sauce, salt and chicken broth and stir to combine.

Set the Egg for 450°F (230°C) direct. With the top and bottom vents wide open, light the fire and close the Egg. When the dome temperature gets up to about 250°F (121°C), about 10 minutes, close the bottom screen. When the dome temperature approaches 450°F (230°C), about 10 minutes, slide the top of the daisy wheel partially closed, keeping it halfway open.

When the dome thermometer reads 450° (230°C), place the wok on the grate that sits on the fire ring. Add 2 tablespoons (30ml) oil and heat until a drop of water dances for one or two seconds on the side of the wok before evaporating. Add the chopped red pepper and stir-fry for one minute; then remove from wok, leaving the oil. Add the garlic and ginger and stir-fry for about 30 seconds before removing from the wok, with the oil. Add 2 tablespoons (30ml) oil and reheat the wok. Add the pork in one layer and stir-fry for 3 minutes. Add the sliced cucumber and continue to stir-fry for another minute. Add the chicken broth mixture, peppers, oil, garlic and ginger back to the wok and continue to stir-fry until the sauce thickens and the cucumber starts to wilt, another one or two minutes. Remove all, add sliced green onion and serve.

CASHEW CHICKEN LETTUCE WRAPS

This recipe has it all: sweet, spicy, savory, crunchy, crispy and juicy. The cornstarch will hold in the chicken's moisture while it cooks. Toasting the cashews first makes them crunchy with a toasted flavor. Word of caution: you will probably need to have ingredients ready for a quick second batch!

MAKES ABOUT 6 SERVINGS

4 boneless, skinless chicken breasts, cut into ¾-inch (2-cm) cubes

2 tablespoons (15g) cornstarch

2 tablespoons (30ml) rice wine or mirin

1 tablespoon (13g) brown sugar

4 tablespoons (60ml) soy sauce

1 tablespoon (15ml) Worcestershire sauce

½ teaspoon salt

¾ cup (175ml) low sodium chicken broth

¼ teaspoon cayenne pepper

1 cup (150g) cashews

4 tablespoons (60ml) vegetable oil, divided

½ cup (32g) sugar snap peas, stems and strings removed, halved lengthwise

2 to 3 carrots, thinly sliced

2 tablespoons (19g) chopped garlic

1 tablespoon (10g) chopped ginger

Several leaves of Boston or iceburg lettuce

Salt and pepper to taste

In a medium bowl, combine the cornstarch and mirin, then add the chicken cubes to coat. In a separate bowl, mix together the brown sugar, soy sauce, Worcestershire sauce, salt, chicken broth and cayenne pepper and stir to combine.

Set up the Egg for 350°F (177°C) direct. With the top and bottom vents wide open, light the fire and close the Egg. When the dome temperature gets up to about 250°F (121°C), about 10 minutes, close the bottom screen. When the dome temperature approaches 350°F (177°C), about 5-10 minutes, slide the top of the daisy wheel partially closed, keeping it ¼ open.

Once the dome temperature is at 350°F (177°C), place a wok on the Egg, sitting on the fire ring. When a drop of water dances on the wok for a second or two, it is hot enough. Add the cashews and toast them for about 5 minutes. Remove the cashews and open the vents to set the Egg at 450° (232°C). Add 2 tablespoons (30ml) of oil, then the peas and carrots and stir-fry for one minute. Remove vegetables from the wok. Add the garlic and ginger to the wok, stir for 30 seconds and remove.

Add remaining 2 tablespoons (30ml) of oil. When it is hot again, add the cubed chicken in one layer and stir-fry for three minutes, browning on all sides. Add the chicken broth mixture, peas, carrots and the garlic, ginger and oil mixture to the wok. Continue to stir-fry until the chicken is cooked, about 2 minutes. Remove and spoon into the lettuce leaves. Add the roasted cashews, salt and pepper to taste and serve.

JULIE'S SHREDDED PORK AND BEANS TACOS

This recipe was contributed by Julie Matison from Verona, Maine. She bought her first Egg fourteen years ago. She now has eight Eggs: an XL, 2 larges, 2 mediums, 1 small and 2 minis. She cooks everything on her Eggs at Eggfests and Egghead Gatherings up and down the East Coast. At your next make-your-own taco party, why not try these? All preparations can be done ahead of time while you and your guests are visiting and enjoying the aromas of the pork loin cooking on the Egg. This recipe makes a small hunk of meat serve a lot of people!

MAKES ABOUT 12 SERVINGS

4 pounds (1800g) boneless pork loin

1 (1-lb [454g]) bag dried pinto beans

1 cup (140g) garlic cloves

2 to 3 teaspoons (6 to 9g) chili powder

1 teaspoon (3g) cumin

24 taco shells or flour or corn tortillas

Taco toppings such as salsa, shredded cheese, sour cream and roasted corn

Set Egg for 350°F to 375°F (177°C to 190°C) indirect. With the top and bottom vents wide open, light the fire and close the Egg. When the dome temperature gets up to about 250°F (121°C), about 10 minutes, close the bottom screen. When the dome temperature approaches 350°F (177°C), about 5-10 minutes, slide the top of the daisy wheel partially closed, keeping it ¼ open.

Place all ingredients except the tortillas in a Dutch oven and add enough water to cover the beans. Cook 2 to 3 hours. Check it once in a while to make sure there is enough water, but you do not want it soupy.

After 2 to 3 hours, the mixture should look like refried beans and the pork should be pretty shredded. Place a scoop of pork and pintos in the center of a taco shell or tortilla and load up with your favorite toppings, such as salsa, shredded cheese, sour cream or roasted corn. Very yummy!

AUNT BETTE'S DUTCH OVEN BAKED BEANS

I found that the perfect way to keep the kitchen cool in the hot summer months is to do all of my baking outdoors. This is a family favorite bean recipe from Aunt Bette that you can tweak by adding your favorite rub or sauce to spice it up.

MAKES 4 TO 6 SERVINGS

1 pound (454g) dry baking beans, such as navy beans

1 (4-ounce [120g]) piece of salt pork

2 tablespoons (20g) chopped onion

3 tablespoons (35g) brown sugar

1 teaspoon (3g) dry mustard

1 teaspoon (6g) salt

¼ cup (60ml) molasses

½ teaspoon (1g) black pepper

⅓ cup (75ml) maple syrup (reserve until beans are almost tender)

Wash the beans and soak them overnight in a large pan, covered by at least 2 inches (5 cm) of water. In the morning, drain and rinse. Return to the pan, cover with water and parboil for 1 to 1½ hours. Place the chopped onion in the bottom of a bean pot or Dutch oven. Add the parboiled beans with liquid, reserving 1 pint (475ml). Place salt pork on top of beans. Mix brown sugar, dry mustard, salt, molasses and pepper with 1 pint (475ml) of the reserved parboiled water and add to the beans. Add more water if needed to cover the beans.

Set the Egg for 300°F (149°C) indirect. With the top and bottom vents wide open, light the fire and close the Egg. When the dome temperature gets up to about 250°F (121°C), about 10 minutes, close the bottom screen. When the dome temperature approaches 300°F (149°C), about 5 minutes, slide the top of the daisy wheel closed, keeping the daisy wheel petals all the way open.

Bake the beans at 300°F (149°C) for 6 hours, or until they are tender. You may need to add more water as the beans cook, so it covers them. Add the maple syrup when they beans are nearly done. My grandfather Wallace taught us that, if you add it too soon, the beans will not soften.

AUNT DOTTIE'S CALICO BEANS

This recipe is from my Aunt Dottie and is a great go-to when you need a side dish to accompany leftover brisket or pork butt. Adding your favorite beans provides color and variety.

MAKES ABOUT 8 SERVINGS

6 slices thick-cut hickory-smoked bacon, sliced into small pieces

¼ cup (40g) diced onion

1 pound (450g) at least 90% lean ground beef

2 (16-ounce [454g]) cans baked beans in sauce

1 (15-ounce [454g]) can kidney beans, drained and rinsed

1 (15-ounce [454g]) can lima beans, drained and rinsed

2 teaspoons (6g) ground mustard

¼ cup (60ml) molasses

¾ cup (151g) brown sugar

¼ cup (60ml) ketchup

Set the Egg for 325°F (163°C) direct. With the top and bottom vents wide open, light the fire and close the Egg. When the dome temperature gets up to about 250°F (121°C), about 10 minutes, close the bottom screen. When the dome temperature approaches 325°F (163°C), about 5 minutes, slide the top of the daisy wheel partially closed, keeping it ¼ open.

In the bottom of a Dutch oven, fry the bacon with the diced onions for 4 to 5 minutes, stirring frequently. Add the ground beef and cook until the beef is browned, about 5 minutes. Add remaining ingredients to the Dutch oven, stir and cover. Cook for 1½ to 2 hours, dome closed and stirring occasionally, to desired consistency. Remove from heat and serve!

CHAPTER 8

INS AND OUTS

CONSTRUCTION, COMPONENTS, ACCESSORIES; USING RUBS, SAUCES AND OTHER CULINARY DELIGHTS

CONSTRUCTION AND COMPONENTS

All sizes of the Big Green Egg are set up the same. The bottom has the lower vent. The top of the Egg is called "the dome" and has an upper vent. The upper vent opening has a ceramic rain cap which should be placed on the Egg when not in use. Add the rain cap and close the lower vent to snuff out the fire.

Between the dome and the bottom is a gasket which helps keep a seal and helps prevent chipping if the Egg is dropped while shut. A hinge assembly attached to the bottom of the dome helps it stay open when raised and keeps the bottom and the dome aligned properly. The seal is important for long cooks. When the fire is fed by fresh air being drafted from the bottom vent up through the charcoal, and then the heat and smoke are drafted up and out the top vent, heat will be drafted through the gasket openings and the dome temperature will not be as high as it should be. A bad gasket can wreak havoc on your lump charcoal, too. During a long cook, a bad seal can make the lump burn out at a much higher temperature than desired, or can make it run out before the meat is cooked. In essence, when the seal is bad, heat bypasses the meat and goes out the gasket gaps.

There are a few common reasons that the gasket might fail. First, when the Egg is new, the cement holding the gasket may not have set well enough. You can re-cement it yourself. You should not do a high-temperature cook the first few times you use your new Egg because flashback can start to burn the gasket. In fact, I don't use my plate setter with the legs down because the heat and possible flashback are directed right at the level of the gasket. Second, air might be escaping because the top and bottom hinges need to be adjusted. I own half a dozen Eggs, and since 2000 I have never replaced a gasket, but that doesn't mean they haven't been burned or haven't worn out. When it is important to have the gasket sealed for a long cook, I will fold a piece of aluminum foil three or four times to a width of about 1 inch (2.5 cm), and use it to cover the curvature of the gasket, which will create a seal when the Egg is closed.

Inside the bottom of the Egg, on top of the firebox, is the fire ring, which holds the burning charcoal and creates a void area for it to burn. The fire box has a hole in the bottom which needs to line up with the bottom vent for the Egg to draft properly. Usually the charcoal is put into the firebox up to the bottom of the fire ring. Too much higher and the combustion chamber area for the charcoal is too limited for even burning, which causes the fire to die out or not get as hot. Together, the firebox and the fire ring create an interior lining where the Egg gets the hottest. Do not use the Egg without the fire ring and firebox in place.

A cast iron fire grate sits in the fire ring near the bottom. Air drafts up through its holes into the charcoal. The side of the firebox also has nickel-sized holes that allow air to draft into the charcoal from the sides. Make sure they are not plugged with ash. (See Chapter 1 on cleaning.)

On top of the fire ring you'll put either a grid for direct cooking or a plate setter for indirect cooking. For direct cooking, I prefer to use a well-seasoned cast iron grate. It retains heat when cold meat is placed on it, and the bars retain the heat that sears the grill marks that tell me that the meat was seared. I always use the plate setter with the legs up and a grid underneath. The extra grid helps catch anything that rolls off the upper grid and gives me the peace of mind in case the plate setter fails. However you set up the plate setter, always put on a leg in the rear of the Egg because that is where the draft is hottest.

Once you have set up on the top of the fire ring, your choices for setups increase. In this book, I explain my setup for each recipe. I always use a foil-lined drip pan on the plate setter when cooking indirectly because I hate getting the plate setter cruddy and because that fat and liquid can burn, creating an acidy smoke. Unless I am doing a multilevel cook, I prefer to cook "up in the dome" on a raised rack on top of the bottom grid, which allows for more even cooking. My preferred pizza or baking setup is a plate setter, legs up, grid on top of the legs, a raised grid on top of the bottom grid, and a pizza stone on the raised grid.

ACCESSORIES

Big Green Egg (www.biggreenegg.com) sells numerous accessories such as griddles and tools for multilevel cooking. Some are half-moon shaped, allowing you to cook at different levels using different techniques.

The Ceramic Grill Store (www.ceramicgrillstore.com) has many accessories for the Egg, including multilevel grid systems for cooking higher in the dome and down below the bottom of the fire ring for indirect cooking. They also carry woks and other accessories that I find very useful in addition to Big Green Egg accessories.

Once you understand the basics for on using your Egg, you will enjoy creating techniques that suit you best.

RUBS AND SAUCES

Dry rubs are essential to great-tasting smoked, roasted and grilled meats and vegetables. You can make your own or select from many in-store and online sources. The best selection of multi-flavored rubs and seasonings comes from Dizzy Pig (www.dizzypigbbq.com). They are a long-time Championship barbecue team using Big Green Eggs. Besides creating excellent rubs, they are a Big Green Egg dealer. You can get their products online or in store.

You can also make your own rubs. There are many recipes available online, and once you get started, you may enjoy creating your own. A few tips are to use turbinado sugar because of its high burning point, and to be careful of the amount of salt you use. Whether you make your own rubs or get them commercially, remember that they have a shelf life. After a period of months, and certainly after a year, most herbs and spices lose their flavor, so all you are left with is salt. I used to make my own rubs, but now I find it easier to buy them commercially and blend them together if necessary.

BASIC BEEF RUB

MAKES ABOUT 1 CUP

4 tablespoons (28g) paprika

1½ tablespoons (22g) kosher salt

1½ tablespoons (5g) fresh ground black pepper

1 tablespoon (9g) garlic powder

1 tablespoon (9g) onion powder

1 teaspoon (2g) cayenne pepper

Mix all ingredients together and store in an airtight container for up to three months.

BASIC PORK RUB

MAKES ABOUT 1 CUP

2 tablespoons (14g) sweet paprika

4 tablespoons (76g) turbinado sugar (we like Sugar in the Raw™)

1½ tablespoons (22g) kosher salt

1 tablespoon (3g) fresh ground black pepper

1 tablespoon (8g) chili powder

1 tablespoon (9g) garlic powder

1 tablespoon (9g) onion powder

1 tablespoon (9g) ground mustard

½ teaspoon (1g) cayenne

Mix all ingredients together and store in an airtight container for up to three months.

BASIC POULTRY RUB

MAKES ABOUT 1 CUP

2 tablespoons (14g) sweet paprika

4 tablespoons (76g) turbinado sugar (we like Sugar in the Raw™)

1½ tablespoons (22g) kosher salt

1 tablespoon (3g) fresh ground black pepper

1 tablespoon (8g) chili powder

1 tablespoon (9g) garlic powder

1 tablespoon (9g) onion powder

1 tablespoon (9g) ground mustard

½ teaspoon cayenne pepper

1 teaspoon (3g) dried oregano

1 teaspoon (3g) dried rosemary

1 teaspoon (3g) dried thyme

Mix all ingredients together and store in an airtight container for up to three months.

Sauces can be vinegar-, mustard-, tomato- or even mayonnaise-based. People's preferences vary regionally. I think Sweet Baby Ray's® sauce is good on pork and chicken and Cattleman's® is good on beef. For competition, I often use sauce from Slabs (www.theslabs.com). Personally, I prefer my barbecue dry, with sauce on the side.

Try substituting different ingredients in my sauce recipes to get that taste you crave. For example, I often sweeten with maple syrup, but you can substitute molasses or honey if you desire. If you like more heat than I do, you can add more cayenne pepper. Let your personal preference guide you.

OTHER KITCHEN ACCESSORIES

Additional kitchen accessories I find useful are a vacuum tumbler for marinating and a vacuum sealer for marinating and for freezing fresh and leftover meats. You can chop cooked pork or brisket, add a little sauce, then vacuum seal it and freeze it. To serve, just reheat the bag in boiling water or the microwave. Barbecue often tastes better the next day; and if frozen, it can be eaten whenever you get the urge!

CHAPTER 9

THE TAIL END

CLEANING, MOVING AND TRANSPORTING; COVERS; CARE OF THE WOK, CAST IRON AND DAISY WHEEL

At many of our demos, someone asks how to clean the Egg. The answer is simple: the Egg is a self-cleaning oven. Get it up to 800°F (427°C) for 30 minutes, and the accumulated crud on the inside of the dome will turn to dust. After 30 minutes or so, close the bottom vent and put the rain cap on the top vent. Do NOT open the Egg. Let it cool for at least one hour. When the dome is cool enough for you to touch, carefully burp the Egg and wipe the inside with a soap-free plastic dish scrubber or sponge. You can use a little spray water to help remove the dust, but it might be a little messier than doing it dry. Do not use a lot of water because it can get into the pores of the ceramic. You can clean the grates in the Egg, too, but the temperature need not be as hot. 400°F (204°C) to 500°F (260°C) will turn any baked-on food to petrified crust, which can be brushed off. I often switch my racks when doing indirect cooking, putting the dirtier one under the plate setter to clean while I do my cook.

If it has been very humid and you haven't used your Egg in a while, mold may form on the grid or in the dome. Check to see if the charcoal is moldy, and if it is, discard it. To clean the mold, follow the same procedure as above.

Because the ceramic of the Egg is porous, grease and moisture will make its way through to the outside, especially after you've used a hot fire to clean the inside. Clean the outside with a non-abrasive scrubbing sponge and water.

MOVING AND TRANSPORTING THE EGG

When you buy an Egg from a dealer, you are given the option to buy an accessory for setting the Egg into or onto. The most common is the Egg "Nest." I recommend the Nest if you are not sure you will have a table nearby and you are going to keep your Egg mostly in one spot. The Nest has casters to allow for careful maneuvering on hard surfaces. Big Green Egg also makes a handle system (Handler) you can attach to the bottom of the Nest and the Egg's hinge assembly. I recommend the Handler if you don't think you will have a table and you plan to move the Egg say, from the garage to the back yard. While the Handler creates an easy way to roll the Egg around, the Egg cannot come out of the nest if you don't unbolt it.

When moving the Egg in the Nest, with or without the handler, always drag the Egg towards you, never push it. The Egg is top-heavy, so it doesn't take much to tip it off balance. If you pull it towards you and it tips and falls, at least you're providing a soft landing spot. I can't say much for your backside or ribs, but you know your priorities!

You can purchase tables to set your Egg into which will provide counter and storage space. Big Green Egg also makes collapsible shelves to attach to the side of the bottom hinge band of the Egg. Some Eggheads prefer to build their Egg into their outdoor patio or make their own table. The Naked Whiz has a picture gallery of over two hundred homemade tables (www.nakedwhiz.com).

Transporting the Egg is not hard, but it requires a bit of planning. The Egg needs to be strapped down so it won't move when you go over a bump. If it is in a table or a Nest in the back of a truck or trailer, tie down both the Egg and the table (or Nest). If you remove the Egg from the table or Nest for transport, make sure it is wrapped with padding under and around it to keep the porcelain from chipping or getting scratched. Big Green Egg makes a carrier which attaches to a Class IV trailer hitch. If you need to, strap the Egg in the front seat with the air bag and ask your spouse to sit in the back. Remember: priorities!

Lifting the Egg can be difficult. It's best to have two or more people. You can put two hands in the bottom vent, balancing the Egg and holding onto the hinge. Don't pull on the hinge when lifting the Egg because the band can slip off and send the dome flying. You can take off the dome and remove the firebox and fire ring to make the Egg lighter. I transport my Eggs all over with the firebox, fire ring, plate setter and grids inside, and I have never had a problem as long as they were strapped down.

COVERS

I cover my Egg outdoors. The rain and snow don't harm the ceramic, but some of the exposed metal parts might corrode. Also, a cover keeps pollen and bird dropping off of my beautiful Egg. I prefer the black fabric premium cover from Big Green Egg. It is heavy, and it won't crack over time like plastic-coated covers will.

CARE OF THE DUTCH OVEN, DAISY WHEEL AND WOK

Cast iron can last for hundreds of years if taken care of properly. The Dutch oven and daisy wheel are both made of cast iron. Many new Dutch ovens are seasoned at purchase, but they may need to be re-seasoned. To protect the seasoning, wash cast iron only in hot water, never with soap. Use a plastic scraper or scrubber to remove burnt-on food, then dry thoroughly and wipe with a little vegetable oil. If the seasoning is worn, or there is any rust, scrub with steel wool and wipe the whole oven inside and out with vegetable oil. Place upside down in a 350°F (177°C) oven or your Egg for one hour, with foil beneath to catch any oil drips. Let cool completely in the oven and repeat 2 more times. Your daisy wheel can be seasoned the same way, by removing any rust and re-seasoning in your oven.

A carbon steel wok needs to be seasoned as well. When new, it may have some oils on it to keep it from corroding. These need to be removed. Use hot, soapy water and a steel wool scouring pad to clean the inside and the outside. This will be the last time you use soap and steel wool in the wok. Dry completely and rub with vegetable oil inside and out. Bake in the oven for 20 minutes at 475°F (246°C). Let it completely cool in the oven and repeat twice more. If your wok has handles that could burn or melt in the oven, you will need to season it on the cook top, coating the inside with oil, heating for 5 minute. Cool and repeat twice.

Do not use steel utensils on cast iron and steel woks because they could scratch and damage the seasoning. Never scrub them with steel wool unless you are re-seasoning them. The more you use a cast iron or a carbon steel wok correctly, the more seasoned and non-stick they will become.

RESOURCES

ACCESSORIES

THE BIG GREEN EGG
www.biggreenegg.com
The "mothership," where you can find product descriptions, information and a dealer locator

THE CERAMIC GRILL STORE
www.ceramicgrillstore.com
Accessories and supplies that can be used on the Big Green Egg

A-MAZE-N PRODUCTS, LLC
www.amazenproducts.com
Cold-smoking accessories and flavored smoking pellets

THERMOWORKS
www.thermoworks.com
Thermapen thermometer

MOXIE
www.drinkmoxie.com

RUBS AND SAUCES

DIZZY PIG BBQ COMPANY
www.dizzypigbbq.com
Rubs, instructional videos, recipes, Big Green Eggs and accessories

THE SLABS
www.theslabs.com

TEXAS PEPPER JELLY
www.texaspepperjelly.com
Grilling and finishing sauces and the best fruit-flavored pepper jelly you will ever taste!

INJECTIONS

BUTCHER BBQ
www.butcherbbq.com
Injections for all meats including beef, pork and poultry

WOOD CHIPS AND CHUNKS

SMOKINLICIOUS
www.smokinlicious.com

ORGANIZATIONS AND INFORMATION

OPERATION BARBECUE RELIEF
www.operationbbqrelief.org
OBR is a non-profit, volunteer disaster response group of families, individuals and barbecue teams who respond to natural disaster emergencies across the United States, providing hot meals to emergency personnel, first responders and those directly affected,. Get involved, whether providing financial assistance, your product or your time. It is a great cause!

KANSAS CITY BARBECUE SOCIETY (KCBS)
www.kcbs.us

NEW ENGLAND BARBECUE SOCIETY (NEBS)
www.nebs.org

THE BIG GREEN EGG FORUM
www.eggheadforum.com
And don't forget The Original Big Green Egg forum at www.greeneggers.com

NAKED WHIZ
www.nakedwhiz.com
Lump charcoal database and resources

ABOUT THE AUTHOR

Eric lives in Bedford, New Hampshire and has been cooking on the Big Green Egg since 2000. In 2006, Eric and his wife Cindi formed the Yabba Dabba Que! Competition Barbecue Team and started competing at barbecue contests throughout the Northeast. In 2007, they were the New England Barbecue Society's (NEBS) Rookie team of the year. In 2009 and 2012, Yabba Dabba Que! competed in the Jack Daniel's Invitational World Championships® in Lynchburg, Tennessee. In 2009, at the American Royal World Series of Barbecue®, the largest competition in the world, they received a perfect score for their crème brûlée.

Eric and Cindi are members of the Kansas City Barbecue Society (KCBS) and the New England Barbecue Society (NEBS). Eric was a three-term Director of NEBS and its recording secretary. Eric has been a KCBS-certified barbecue judge since 2006.

Eric and Cindi have attended and cooked at several Eggfests in Waldorf, Maryland and Brentwood, New Hampshire. For the past five years, they have been performing Big Green Egg demonstrations for Tarantin Industries at dealerships throughout New England and New York.

When he is not cooking on his Eggs, Eric works as a licensed land surveyor.

ACKNOWLEDGMENTS

I would first like to thank my wife Cindi for her love and support and for encouraging me to write this book. I also thank her for typing the manuscript and for putting up with me during all our barbecue escapades.

Thanks to all who furnished recipes: Michele and Tom Perelka of the Lo'-N-Slo' Competition BBQ Team, Wendy and Tim Boucher of the Feeding Friendz Competition BBQ Team, Mike "Sully" Sullivan from the lunchmeat Competition BBQ Team, Nancy and Chuck Helwig of the Smokin' Aces Competition BBQ Team, fellow Eggheads Kim and Ginny Youngblood and Julie Matison, my daughter Rebecca, my mother Madeline, Aunt Bette, Aunt Dottie and my cousins Karen and Tim.

Thank you to Ken Goodman for his beautiful photography, which makes the recipes look as good as they taste.

Special thanks to Tim and Wendy Boucher and Bill and Shaune Gillespie for helping with the photo shoot.

Thank you to Sharry Morse for keeping my manuscript organized. Thanks also to Will Kiester and Marissa Giambelluca and everyone at Page Street Publishing.

And lastly, thank you to all who have judged my food: family, friends and strangers.

INDEX

A

ABT: A Beautiful Thing, 87, 90, *90–91*

accessories, 207, 209

agave, 70, 107

allspice, 41, 74, 123, 153, 165

almonds, 149

A-Maze-N Pellet smoker, 159, 163

American Royal Invitational, 7

ancho chili powder, 61

apple cider, 21–23, 24–26, 35–36, 48, 118

apple cider vinegar, 30, 35–36, 49, 61, 106, 111, 173, 174

apple juice, 21–23, 34, 48, 118

apple pie filling, 77

Apple Pie Pork Loin, *76*, 77

apples, 35–36, 123, 189

applewood, 59

apricots, 89

Arborio rice, 84

asparagus, 137

    Grilled Garlic Asparagus, *100–101*, 101

Aunt Bette's Dutch Oven Baked Beans, 201

Aunt Dottie's Calico Beans, 202, *203*

Award-Winning Coffee-Encrusted Pork Tenderloin, *114*, 115

B

Baby Back Ribs, 34

bacon, 73, 74, 96, 123, 180, 195

    ABT: A Beautiful Thing, 87, 90, *90–91*

    Aunt Dottie's Calico Beans, 202, *203*

    Buckboard Bacon, 165

    Canadian Bacon, 164

    Cindi's Bacon-Wrapped Dried Apricots with Cranberry Glaze, *88*, 89

    First Place Armadillo Rats, 90, *90–91*

    Homemade Bacon, 160, *160–161*

    Spicy, Corny Bacon Fritters, 180, *180–181*

    Stir-Fried Brussels Sprouts with Bacon, 193, *193*

    Stir-Fry Summer Succotash, *194–195*, 195

baking, 131–157

    Aunt Bette's Dutch Oven Baked Beans, 201

    Blueberry Buckle, *144*, 145

    Blueberry Scones, 154, *155*

    Bourbon Pecan Pie, *140*, 141

    Cousin Karen's Soft Pretzels, 157

    Cranberry Oatmeal Cookies, 156

    Hermits, *152–153*, 153

    Italian Cold Cut Stromboli, 132, *133*

    Kim's Mexican Chicken Casserole, 135

    Maple Crème Brûlée, 142, *142–143*

    Maple Skillet Cornbread, 134

    Mixed Fruit Crostada, *148*, 149

    Peach Bread Pudding with Rum Sauce, 138, *139*

    Scotch Eggs, 182

    Smokin' Aces Pizza, *136*, 137

    Southern Corn Pudding, 150, *151*

    Spinach and Feta Stuffed Bread, 146, *147*

    Steak and Cheese Stuffed Bread, 146

balsamic vinegar, 98, 99

Barbecued Beef Back Ribs, 44, *45*

Barbecued Bologna, 86

Barbecued Jerk Chicken, *40*, 41

barbecue sauce, 21–23

barbecuing

    Baby Back Ribs, 34

    Barbecued Beef Back Ribs, 44, *45–46*

    Barbecued Bologna, 86

    Barbecued Jerk Chicken, *40*, 41

    Beef Brisket Burnt Ends, 32, *33*

    Big Green Egg Pastrami, 47

    Competition Beef Brisket, 27–29, *28–29*

    Competition Boston Pork Butt, 21–23, *22–23*

    Competition Pork Ribs, 24–26, *25–26*

    Lo'-N-'Slo BBQ Roasted Turkey, 35–36

    Maryland-Style Pit Beef, 37, *38*

    Slow Roasted Pork Steaks, 48

Basic Beef Burgers, 122

Basic Beef Rub, 208

Basic Pork Rub, 208

Basic Poultry Rub, 209

basil, 94, 195

bay leaves, 35–36, 106

beans, 200

    Aunt Bette's Dutch Oven Baked Beans, 201

    Aunt Dottie's Calico Beans, 202, *203*

Becky's Jicama Salad, 107
beef, 19, 47, 93. *See also specific cuts*
    Basic Beef Burgers, 122
    Deep-Fried Brisket Empanadas, *184–185*, 185
    Grilled Chicken or Beef Teriyaki, *126*, 127
    Maryland-Style Pit Beef, 37, *38*
beef back ribs, 44, *45–46*
beef brisket, 19, 20
    The Best Beef Brisket Hash, 174, *175*
    Big Green Egg Pastrami, 47
    Competition Beef Brisket, 27–29, *28–29*
    Spicy Beef Jerky, 166, *167*
Beef Brisket Burnt Ends, 32, *33*
beef broth, 174
beef jerky, 166, *167*
Beef Rub, 27–29, 37, 44, 62, 69, 73, 86, 208
beef short ribs, *68*, 69
beef tenderloin, 128, *129*
beer, 30, 44
Belgian endive, 99
bell peppers, 49, 84, 107, 195, 196
The Best Beef Brisket Hash, 174, *175*
Big Green Egg, 7
    accessories, 207
    cleaning, 211
    components, 205–206, *206*
    construction, 205–206, *206*
    covers, 212
    moving, 212
    transporting, 212
Big Green Egg Pastrami, 47
Big Green Eggplant Parmigiana, 94, *95*
blackberries, 149
black pepper, 47, 79, 98, 177, 208, 209
blade steak, Marinated Blade Steak, 111
blueberries, 145, 149, 154
    Blueberry Buckle, *144*, 145
    Blueberry Scones, 154, *155*
Blueberry Buckle, *144*, 145
Blueberry Scones, 154, *155*
bologna, 86
bourbon, 73, 98, 117, 141
Bourbon-Glazed Carrots, 98
Bourbon Moxie™ Meatballs, *72*, 73
Bourbon Pecan Pie, *140*, 141
Bourbon Soy Flank Steak, *116*, 117

bread
    Spinach and Feta Stuffed Bread, 146, *147*
    Steak and Cheese Stuffed Bread, 146
bread crumbs, 56, 73, 105, 170, 179, 182
bread dough, 146
bread pudding, 138
Brisket Rub, 32
brown mustard, 42
brown sugar, 42, 47, 61, 65, 66, 96, 111, 115, 118, 121, 127, 138,
    141, 145, 153, 156, 160, 164, 166, 189, 196, 199, 201, 202
brussels sprouts, 193
Buckboard Bacon, 165
burgers
    Basic Beef Burgers, 122
    Spicy Apple Pork Burgers, 123
burping, 12
butter, 35–36, 61, 73, 98, 112, 128, 138, 141, 145, 149, 150, 153,
    154, 156, 173
buttermilk, 177, 180, 183, 186

C
cabbage, 78, 174
    Cindi's Slaw, 49
Canadian Bacon, 164
carrots, 98, 107, 174, 199
Cashew Chicken Lettuce Wraps, *198*, 199
cashews, 199
casseroles, 135
catfish, 177
cayenne pepper, 61, 65, 66, 74, 93, 96, 117, 170, 180, 183, 195, 199,
    208, 209
Cedar-Planked Salmon, 66, *67*
celery, 73
celery seed, 49
Ceramic Grill Store, 207
Championship Coffee-Encrusted Lamb Chops, *120*, 121
charcoal, 9–12, *10–11*, 16–17, 206
cheddar cheese, 93, 135, 176
cheese, 146. *See also specific cheeses*
    Smoked Cheese, *162–163*, 163
Cheesy Stuffed Chicken Breast, 58
cherry chunks, 17
chicken, 58
    Barbecued Jerk Chicken, *40*, 41
    Cashew Chicken Lettuce Wraps, *198*, 199
    Competition Smoked Chicken, 31

Grilled Chicken or Beef Teriyaki, *126*, 127
Kim's Mexican Chicken Casserole, 135
    raw, 13
    Spicy Chicken Wings, *60*, 61
    Spicy Fried Chicken, 183
    Tequila Lime Chicken Thighs, 70, *70–71*
chicken broth, 74, 84, 135, 199
Chicken Rub, 31, 80, 83
chili, 176
chili oil, 55
chili peppers, 41, 70, 74, 83, 87, 90, 106, 107, 134, 135, 180
chili powder, 61, 93, 102, 112, 200, 208, 209
chimney charcoal starters, 9, 11
chipotle peppers in adobo sauce, 124, 135, 166
chips, 17, 52
chorizo, 84, 146
chunks, 17
Cider-Brined Pork Chops with Peach Salsa, 118, *119*
cilantro, 70, 78, 107, 135
Cindi's Bacon-Wrapped Dried Apricots with Cranberry Glaze, *88*, 89
Cindi's Deep-Fried Coconut Shrimp, *178*, 179
Cindi's Slaw, 49
cinnamon, 41, 138, 145, 153, 156, 189
clams, 84
cleaning, 211
cloves, 35–36, 41
Coca-Cola©, 124
coconut, 179
cod, 78
coffee, 115, 121
Cointreau, 115
Competition Beef Brisket, 27–29, *28–29*
Competition Boston Pork Butt, 21–23, *22–23*
Competition Pork Ribs, 24–26, *25–26*
Competition Smoked Chicken, 31
components, 205–206, *206*
construction, 205–206, *206*
cookies, 156
corn, 102, 150, 180
cornbread, 134
corned beef, 47
cornmeal, 134, 177, 180, 186
cornstarch, 179, 196, 199
cotija cheese, 102
Cousin Karen's Soft Pretzels, 157

covers, 212
crab cakes, 170, *171*
crabmeat, 170
cranberries, 89, 138, 156
Cranberry Oatmeal Cookies, 156
cream, 138, 142, 154, 189
cream cheese, 58, 176
crème brûlée, 142, *142–143*
cross-contamination, 13
cucumbers, 196
cumin, 93, 107, 135, 200
curing, 159–167
    Buckboard Bacon, 165
    Canadian Bacon, 164
    Homemade Bacon, 160, *160–161*
curing salts, 47

D
daisy wheels, 13, *14–15*, 15, 213
Deep-Fried Brisket Empanadas, *184–185*, 185
Deep-Fried Catfish, 177, *177*
deep frying, 169–203
    Cindi's Deep-Fried Coconut Shrimp, *178*, 179
    Deep-Fried Brisket Empanadas, *184–185*, 185
    Deep-Fried Catfish, 177, *177*
    Double Crunch Fried Pickles, 186, *186–187*
    "Honey Jack" Apple Nachos, *188*, 189
    Pork Cracklin's, 192
    Scotch Eggs, 182
    Spicy, Corny Bacon Fritters, 180, *180–181*
    Spicy Fried Chicken, 183
    Unassuming Fried Plantains, 190, *191*
Dijon mustard, 61, 66, 170
dips, 176
direct cooking, 206
Dizzy Pig, 207
domes, 205, 206
Double Crunch Fried Pickles, 186, *186–187*
dressings, 99
drip pans, 11, *11*, 12, 20, 52
dry rubs, 19, 207
    Basic Beef Rub, 208
    Basic Pork Rub, 208
    Basic Poultry Rub, 209
Dutch ovens, 169, 213

E

eggplant, 94, *95*

egg rolls, 97

eggs, 73, 134, 138, 141, 142, 145, 153, 156, 174, 179, 180, 182

electric fire starters, 11

empanadas, *184–185*, 185

F

fat, rendering, 12

feta cheese, 146

fireboxes, 159, 206

fire grates, 206

fire rings, 206

First Place Armadillo Rats, 90, *90–91*

fish, 84

    Cedar-Planked Salmon, 66, *67*

    Deep-Fried Catfish, 177, *177*

    Miso Mango Fish Tacos, 78

    raw, 13

flank steak

    Bourbon Soy Flank Steak, *116*, 117

    Grilled Chicken or Beef Teriyaki, *126*, 127

flashbacks, 12, 110

foil, 20, 52

food paraffin fire starters, 11

food safety, 13

food temperature, 13. *See also* temperature

food thermometers, 13

Fritacos Fantásticos, *92*, 93

fruit, 149. *See also specific fruit*

fruitwood, 17, 160, 164, 165

frying, 170, *171*. *See also* deep frying; stir-frying

G

garlic, 35–36, 39, 41, 47, 55, 56, 58, 70, 73, 74, 77, 84, 94, 99, 101, 105, 106, 111, 117, 118, 123, 124, 127, 164, 166, 173, 193, 195, 196, 199, 200

garlic powder, 65, 93, 98, 112, 115, 121, 135, 165, 174, 177, 183, 186, 208, 209

Garlic Sausage, 91

Garlic Sausage Fatties, 74, *75*

gaskets, 205

ginger, 41, 78, 111, 127, 196, 199

gloves, 12

gouda cheese, 122

green beans, 195

green chilis, 135

green onions, 41, 55, 196. *See also* scallions

Griddled Crab Cakes, 170, *171*

griddles, 207

griddling, 169–203

grids, 11–13, 16, 20, 51–52, 109, 131, 206

Grilled Asian Marinated Pork Belly, *54–55*, 55

Grilled Belgian Endive with Balsamic Dressing, 99

Grilled Chicken or Beef Teriyaki, *126*, 127

Grilled Garlic Asparagus, *100–101*, 101

Grilled Mexican Corn on the Cob, 102, *103*

grilling, 19, 109–129

    Award-Winning Coffee-Encrusted Pork Tenderloin, *114*, 115

    Basic Beef Burgers, 122

    Bourbon Soy Flank Steak, *116*, 117

    Championship Coffee-Encrusted Lamb Chops, *120*, 121

    Cider-Brined Pork Chops with Peach Salsa, 118, *119*

    Grilled Asian Marinated Pork Belly, *54–55*, 55

    Grilled Belgian Endive with Balsamic Dressing, 99

    Grilled Chicken or Beef Teriyaki, *126*, 127

    Grilled Garlic Asparagus, *100–101*, 101

    Grilled Mexican Corn on the Cob, 102, *103*

    Marinated Blade Steak, 111

    Roasted Beef Tenderloin, 128, *129*

    Spicy Apple Pork Burgers, 123

    Spicy Rib Eye Steak, 112, *113*

    Sully's Marinated Steak Tips, 124, *125*

Grill-Roasted Beef Short Ribs, *68*, 69

Grill-Roasted Pork Braciole, 56, *56–57*

ground beef, 93

ground chuck

    Basic Beef Burgers, 122

    Bourbon Moxie™ Meatballs, *72*, 73

ground mustard, 208, 209

ground pork, 123

H

habanero peppers, 41

haddock, 78

half-and-half, 138

ham

    Italian Cold Cut Stromboli, 132, *133*

    Smoked Ham, 42, *42–43*

hand-held gas torches, 9

hardwood lump charcoal, 17

hash, 174

Hermits, *152*, 153
hickory, 17
Homemade Bacon, *160–161*, 161
honey, 24–26, 61, 65, 98, 99, 111, 117
"Honey Jack" Apple Nachos, *188*, 189
honey whiskey, 189
horseradish, 39
hot pepper flakes, 55
hot sauce, 65, 176

I

indirect cooking, 16, 206, 207
indirect roasting, 51–52
injection, 27–29
Italian Cold Cut Stromboli, 132, *133*

J

Jack Daniel's Invitational World Championship of Barbecue, 7
jalapeño peppers, 70, 74, 83, 87, 90, 106, 107, 134, 180
jerky, 166, *167*
jicama, 107
Julie's Shredded Pork and Bean Tacos, 200

K

Kansas City Barbecue Society (KCBS), 7
ketchup, 65, 202
kidney beans, 202
Kim's Mexican Chicken Casserole, 135

L

lamb
    Championship Coffee-Encrusted Lamb Chops, *120*, 121
    Tender Roasted Rack of Lamb, 79
lemon juice, 39, 58, 66, 101, 105, 170, 173
lemons, 35–36, 84, 189
lettuce, 65, 199
lighter fluid, 9
lighting instructions, 9–12
lima beans, 202
lime juice, 65, 70, 78, 83, 102, 118, 149
limes, 35–36, 41
loin rib chops, 118
Lo'-N-'Slo BBQ Roasted Turkey, 35–36
lump charcoal, 9, 17

M

mangoes, 78
maple chunks, 17, 59
Maple Crème Brûlée, 142, *143*
Maple Skillet Cornbread, 134
maple syrup, 21–23, 42, 134, 138, 142, 165, 189, 201
Mapp gas, 9
marinades, 30
Marinated Blade Steak, 111
Maryland-Style Pit Beef, 37, *38*
mayonnaise, 39, 65, 78, 102, 170
meatballs, *72*, 73
meats
    barbecue, 19 (*see also specific meats*)
    raw, 13
mesquite, 17
milk, 134, 145, 180
mirin, 127, 196, 199
Miso Mango Fish Tacos, 78
miso paste, 78
Mitchell, Cindi, 7
Mitchell, Eric C., 7
Mixed Fruit Crostada, *148*, 149
molasses, 153, 165, 201, 202
Moxie™, 73
mozzarella cheese, 94, 137, 176
mushrooms, 58, 73
mustard, 61, 66, 86, 123, 170, 174, 201, 202, 208, 209
mustard seed, 49

N

nachos, 189
Naked Whiz, 17
navy beans, 201
nectarines, 87, 90, *90–91*, 149
Nest, 212
New England Barbecue Society (NEBS), 7
nutmeg, 41, 74, 150, 156, 189

O

oats, 156
onion powder, 58, 65, 93, 112, 115, 121, 177, 183, 186, 208, 209
onions, 35–36, 49, 65, 73, 78, 84, 93, 105, 106, 107, 118, 135, 164, 170, 174, *184–185*, 195, 201. *See also specific kinds of onion*
orange juice, 35–36, 58, 70
orange marmalade, 115

oranges, 35–36, 41
oregano, 35–36, 93, 106, 107, 209

P

paella, 84, *85*
paprika, 61, 65, 84, 93, 107, 112, 208, 209
Parmesan cheese, 56, 58, 94, 105
parsley, 35–36, 56, 58, 84, 128, 170, 173
parsnips, 174
pastrami, 47
Peach Bread Pudding with Rum Sauce, 138, *139*
peaches, 118, 138
peach salsa, 118
peas, 199
pecan, 17
pecans, 138, 141
pecan wood, 69
pellets, 159
peppercorns, 35–36, 77, 106, 164
Peppered Pig Candy, 96
pepper jack cheese, 146
pepperoncini, 56
pesto sauce, 137
pickles, 186
pickling spice, 47
pies, Bourbon Pecan Pie, *140*, 141
pinto beans, 200
pit masters, 11
pizza, *136*, 137
plantains, 190, *191*
plate setters, 11, *11*, 13, 51–52, 206
po' boys, 65
pork, 19, 97. *See also specific cuts*
    Spicy Apple Pork Burgers, 123
pork belly, 192
    Grilled Asian Marinated Pork Belly, *54–55*, 55
    Homemade Bacon, 160
pork butts, 19, 20
    Competition Boston Pork Butt, 21–23, *22–23*
pork chops, Cider-Brined Pork Chops with Peach Salsa, 118, *119*
Pork Cracklin's, 192
pork loin
    Apple Pie Pork Loin, *76*, 77
    Canadian Bacon, 164
    Julie's Shredded Pork and Bean Tacos, 200
pork marinade, 21–23

pork ribs
    Competition Pork Ribs, 24–26, *25–26*
    Slow-Roasted Country-Style Pork Ribs, 59
Pork Rub, 21–23, 24–26, 34, 48, 59, 74, 77, 91, 118, 208
pork shoulder, 19, 20, 165
    Garlic Sausage Fatties, 74, *75*
    Grill-Roasted Pork Braciole, 56, *56–57*
    Stir-Fried Garlic Pork with Cucumber, 196, *197*
pork steaks, Slow Roasted Pork Steaks, 48
pork tenderloin, Award-Winning Coffee-Encrusted Pork Tenderloin, *114*, 115
potatoes, 174
Poultry Rub, 209
pretzels, 157
Primetime Rib Roast, 62, *63*
provolone cheese, 132, 176
pudding, 150
pulled pork, 97
Pulled Pork Egg Rolls, 97, *97*

Q

queso fresco, 102
quick-cure salt, 160, 164, 165

R

raisins, 153
raspberries, 149
raspberry jam, 83
Rebecca's Pickled Onions, 106
red onions, 107, 118, 170
red pepper flakes, 166
red pepper relish, 137
red peppers, roasted, 132
red wine vinegar, 106
rib eye steak, 112, *113*
rib roast, 62, *63*
ribs, 20, 34, 56
    Barbecued Beef Back Ribs, 44, *45–46*
    Competition Pork Ribs, 24–26, *25–26*
    Slow-Roasted Country-Style Pork Ribs, 59
    Stir-Fried Garlic Pork with Cucumber, 196, *197*
rice, 84, 135
rice wine, 196, 199
rice wine vinegar, 55, 78
Rick's Sinful Marinade, 27–29, 30, 69
Roasted Beef Tenderloin, 128, *129*

Roasted Boneless Turkey Breast, 80, *80–81*
roasting, 20, 51–107
    ABT: A Beautiful Thing, 87, 90, *90–91*
    Apple Pie Pork Loin, *76*, 77
    Barbecued Bologna, 86
    Big Green Eggplant Parmigiana, 94, 95
    Bourbon-Glazed Carrots, 98
    Bourbon Moxie™ Meatballs, *72*, 73
    Cedar-Planked Salmon, 66, *67*
    Cheesy Stuffed Chicken Breast, 58
    Cindi's Bacon-Wrapped Dried Apricots with Cranberry Glaze, *88*, 89
    First Place Armadillo Rats, 90, *90–91*
    Fritacos Fantásticos, *92*, 93
    Garlic Sausage Fatties, 74, *75*
    Grilled Asian Marinated Pork Belly, *54–55*
    Grilled Belgian Endive with Balsamic Dressing, 99
    Grilled Garlic Asparagus, *100–101*, 101
    Grilled Mexican Corn on the Cob, 102, *103*
    Grill-Roasted Beef Short Ribs, *68*, 69
    Grill-Roasted Pork Braciole, 56, *56–57*
    Miso Mango Fish Tacos, 78
    Peppered Pig Candy, 96
    Primetime Rib Roast, 62, *63*
    Pulled Pork Egg Rolls, 97, *97*
    Rebecca's Pickled Onions, 106
    Roasted Boneless Turkey Breast, 80, *80–81*
    Seafood Paella, 84, *85*
    Slow-Roasted Country-Style Pork Ribs, 59
    Spicy Chicken Wings, *60*, 61
    Spicy Shrimp Po' Boy, *64*, 65
    Tender Roasted Rack of Lamb, 79
    Tender Turkey Tenderloin with Raspberry-Lime Glaze, *82*, 83
    Tequila Lime Chicken Thighs, 70, *70–71*
    Zucchini Boats, *104*, 105
rosemary, 35–36, 79, 209
rubs, 207
rum, 138

S
safety, 12–13
saffron, 84
sage, 35–36
salads, 107. *See also* slaw
salami, 56, 132, *133*
salmon, 66, *67*

salsa, 118, 176
salt pork, 195
    Aunt Bette's Dutch Oven Baked Beans, 201
    Stir-Fry Summer Succotash, *194–195*, 195
sandwiches. *See also* burgers
    Maryland-Style Pit Beef, 37, *38*
    Spicy Shrimp Po' Boy, *64*, 65
sauces, 39, 207
sausage, 105, 182
scallions, 118, 123, 195. *See also* green onions
scallops, 173
scones, 154, *155*
Scotch Eggs, 182
Seafood Paella, 84, *85*
Seared and Sauced Sea Scallops, *172*, 173
searing, 109–110
    Seared and Sauced Sea Scallops, *172*, 173
sesame oil, 55, 127
sesame seeds, 55
shallots, 58, 128, 173, 193
shrimp, 84
    Cindi's Deep-Fried Coconut Shrimp, *178*, 179
    Spicy Shrimp Po' Boy, *64*, 65
sirloin roast, 37
skewers, 127
slaw, 49, 97
Slow-Roasted Country-Style Pork Ribs, 59
Slow Roasted Pork Steaks, 48
Smoked Cheese, *162–163*
Smoked Ham, 42, *43*
Smokin' Aces Pizza, *136*, 137
smoking, 159–167
    Buckboard Bacon, 165
    Canadian Bacon, 164
    Competition Smoked Chicken, 31
    Smoked Cheese, *162–163*, 163
    Smoked Ham, 42, *42–43*
    Spicy Beef Jerky, 166, *167*
smoking pellets, 159
sour cream, 93, 135
Southern Corn Pudding, 150, *151*
soy sauce, 55, 58, 111, 115, 117, 127, 166, 196, 199
Spicy, Corny Bacon Fritters, 180, *180–181*
Spicy Apple Pork Burgers, 123
Spicy Beef Jerky, 166, *167*
Spicy Chicken Wings, *60*, 61

Spicy Fried Chicken, 183
Spicy Rib Eye Steak, 112, *113*
Spicy Shrimp Po' Boy, *64*, 65
Spinach and Feta Stuffed Bread, 146, *147*
steak, 146
    Bourbon Soy Flank Steak, *116*, 117
    Marinated Blade Steak, 111
    Spicy Rib Eye Steak, 112, *113*
    Steak and Cheese Stuffed Bread, 146
Steak and Cheese Stuffed Bread, 146
steak tips, 124, *125*
Stir-Fried Brussels Sprouts with Bacon, 193, *193*
Stir-Fried Garlic Pork with Cucumber, 196, *197*
stir-frying, 169, 169–203
    Cashew Chicken Lettuce Wraps, *198*, 199
    Stir-Fried Brussels Sprouts with Bacon, 193, *193*
    Stir-Fried Garlic Pork with Cucumber, 196, *197*
    Stir-Fry Summer Succotash, *194–195*, 195
Stir-Fry Summer Succotash, *194*, 195
stromboli, 132
sugar, 74, 78, 138, 142, 145, 149, 153, 156, 173, 208, 209
sugar snap peas, 199
Sully's Damn Dip, 176
Sully's Marinated Steak Tips, 124, *125*

T
tacos
    Julie's Shredded Pork and Bean Tacos, 200
    Miso Mango Fish Tacos, 78
Tarantin Industries, 7
temperature, 11–12, 13
    achieving, 15–17
    barbecuing, 20
    for deep frying, 169
    for indirect cooks, 20
    low, 19
    searing, 109–110
    for stir-frying, 169
    temperature control, 13
tenderloin, 19
Tender Roasted Rack of Lamb, 79
Tender Turkey Tenderloin with Raspberry-Lime Glaze, *82*, 83
tequila, 70
Tequila Lime Chicken Thighs, 70, *70–71*
Thermopen, 13
Thermo Works, 13

thyme, 35–36, 41, 58, 84, 195, 209
Tiger Sauce, 37, 39, 62
tomatoes, 65, 84, 94, 118, 135, 137
Tombari, Bill, 7
Tombari, Sandy, 7
tools, 207
triple sec, 115
turkey
    Italian Cold Cut Stromboli, 132, *133*
    Lo'-N-'Slo BBQ Roasted Turkey, 35–36
    Roasted Boneless Turkey Breast, 80, *80–81*
    Tender Turkey Tenderloin with Raspberry-Lime Glaze, *82*, 83
turnips, 174

U
Unassuming Fried Plantains, 190, *191*

V
vacuum tumblers, 209
vanilla beans, 142
vanilla extract, 138, 141, 156
vent holes, 9
vents, 12, 205
vinegar, 49. *See also specific vinegars*

W
walnuts, 153
whiskey, 189
white vinegar, 41, 49
Wicked Good Charcoal, 17
woks, 169, 213
wood chunks, 11, *11*, 17, 19, 52, 165. *See also specific kinds of wood chunks*
Worcestershire sauce, 30, 44, 73, 166, 196, 199

Y
yellow mustard, 21–23, 27–29, 34, 44, 48, 59

Z
zucchini, 105
Zucchini Boats, *104*, 105